Three Years After

Next Steps in the War on Terror

David Aaron, editor

RAND
CORPORATION

This publication results from RAND's continuing program of self-initiated research. Support for such research is provided, in part, by donors and by the independent research and development provisions of RAND's contracts for the operation of its U.S. Department of Defense federally funded research and development centers.

ISBN 0-8330-3752-8

The RAND Corporation is a nonprofit research organization providing objective analysis and effective solutions that address the challenges facing the public and private sectors around the world. RAND's publications do not necessarily reflect the opinions of its research clients and sponsors.

Published 2005 by the RAND Corporation
1776 Main Street, P.O. Box 2138, Santa Monica, CA 90407-2138
1200 South Hayes Street, Arlington, VA 22202-5050
201 North Craig Street, Suite 202, Pittsburgh, PA 15213-1516
RAND URL: http://www.rand.org/
To order RAND documents or to obtain additional information, contact
Distribution Services: Telephone: (310) 451-7002;
Fax: (310) 451-6915; Email: order@rand.org

Preface

This volume is the product of a conference sponsored by the RAND Corporation in Washington, D.C., on September 8, 2004. Entitled *Three Years After: Next Steps in the War on Terror,* it presented the results of several cutting-edge studies as well as commentary on recent counterterrorism issues. The presentations were supported by funds from RAND's corporate resources, as well as work done under contract for the U.S. Air Force, the Office of the Secretary of Defense, the U.S. intelligence community, and foreign governments. The resulting volume provides summaries of the presentations and panels, in addition to the text of the luncheon address by Deputy Secretary of Defense Paul Wolfowitz, which is attached as an appendix.

This publication results from the RAND's continuing program of self-initiated research. Support for such research is provided, in part, by donors and by the independent research and development provisions of RAND's contracts for the operation of its U.S. Department of Defense federally funded research and development centers.

The principal organizer of the conference was Ambassador David L. Aaron, who also prepared this volume. For more information, contact Ambassador Aaron by email at daaron@rand.org; by phone at (310) 393-0411 x7782; or by mail at The RAND Corporation, 1776 Main Street, Santa Monica, CA 90407-2138.

Contents

CHAPTER ONE

Introduction

Three years after 9/11, many studies by scores of institutions have been undertaken to find ways of dealing with the challenge of terrorism. With the approach of the third anniversary of the attack on the World Trade Center and the Pentagon, the RAND Corporation decided to hold a conference to share the results of its recent studies with government officials, military officers, congressional staff, foundations and nongovernmental organizations (NGOs), foreign embassy representatives, and the public at large.

RAND started working on the issue of terrorism in 1972, after the attack on the Israeli athletes at the Munich Olympics. The first person at RAND to pursue research on this topic was Brian Michael Jenkins, whom you will be hearing from today. He was in charge of the program that was called "Terrorism and Subnational Conflict." Under his leadership, a database called "The Chronology of Terrorism" was started in 1972, with the data going back to 1968. That database continues to be updated and available to the public. We felt that this was a field that was lacking in empirical evidence and that if we had evidence we could begin to learn some new things.

And indeed we did. Bruce Hoffman, who we are also going to hear from today, began using this chronology in his research, and he noticed in the early '90s changes in the patterns of terrorism. In particular, he noted that while the number of terrorist events was declining, the lethality was growing. Through his research, he connected this to a change in the objectives of terrorism—in particular, the growth in terrorism with religious and millennial motivations. He and colleagues from RAND, with Air Force sponsorship, published a study in 1999 called *Countering the New Terrorism*, which was an effort to address how we could deal with this problem.

RAND principally works for clients (65 percent of which are in the federal government) who pay us directly under contract or grants for projects that they and we agree are worth pursuing. Ninety-five percent of our work is done on that basis, while 5 percent is self-initiated, supported by fees earned on our contracts, from donations mainly from individuals, or from endowment earnings. That money enables us to do independent projects and has allowed us to present this conference.

During the earliest days of working on terrorism, client interest in Washington varied. There were years when interest was intense, and then years when interest just vanished. That began to change in the '90s, especially after the phenomenon of the new terrorism, or al Qaeda, became obvious. Today, we have 50 projects that are funded by our clients.

Our work on this issue is in four broad categories: (1) Understanding the Nature of the Terrorist Threat; (2) Taking Direct Action Against Terrorists and Terrorist Organizations; (3) Seeking to Reduce the Support for Terrorists, concerned with the supply of recruits, the finances, and the like; and (4) Protecting the Homeland. We'll be presenting today a selection from these categories, and given the amount of work we do on this area I do want to stress that it is but a selection. Very many important areas are not included because of the limited time available, including our research on public health and terrorism. If this conference works, we'll come back again and provide another selection, focusing more closely on homeland security.

I mentioned this work comes from clients and donors and I want to take this opportunity to thank them for their support. I hope you'll conclude from this selection of topics that RAND is living up to its core values of quality and objectivity. We look forward to your reactions and to the discussion. Thank you.

James A. Thomson
President and CEO
The RAND Corporation

CHAPTER TWO
The Jihadists' Operational Code

Brian Michael Jenkins

Knowing the adversary is a key to developing sound responses to security challenges. Such research has ample precedent. Before WWII, the German General Staff played out their plans for the invasion of France against German officers steeped in French military thinking. For their part, American officers read the works of German strategists and, later in the 1960s, the writings of Mao Tse-tung, Che Guevara, and Carlos Marighella. In 1951, during the Cold War, RAND published a book written by Nathan Leites, *The Operational Code of the Politburo*, which sought to understand the dynamics of Soviet decisionmaking. It spawned generations of "Kremlinologists."

Interestingly, many choose not to understand terrorists, often dismissing them as crazy fanatics. Initial efforts to understand their behavior focused on their individual pathology—the "terrorist personality." To go beyond this could be politically dangerous. It might confer a certain legitimacy on the terrorists; it risks getting into debates on causes and political goals, which objective definitions sought to avoid. It even could be seen as exhibiting a lack of antiterrorist zeal.

But without justifying terrorism, a broader examination of the terrorists' operational perspectives would be productive in several ways. It would suggest analytical frameworks for intelligence, challenge our own presumptions, and possibly open up different approaches for counterterrorist efforts.

One can start by asking several questions about terrorists:

- What is their worldview? Their view of war? Their concept of fighting?

- How do they think about strategy?

- How do they view operations?

- What is their operational code?

- What might make their heart race?

- Are there things they would not do?

- How do they plan?

- How do they recruit?

- How might they assess their current situation?

- How do they look at the future?

According to the Jihadists exemplified by al Qaeda, Islam is in mortal danger from the West. The source of this threat is the United States. Conflating events hundreds of years apart, they see Americans as the new Mongols. U.S. military bases throughout the Middle East, in the Persian Gulf, and Central Asia provide proof.

America supports the Zionists, no different from the invading Crusaders of the 11th century, who occupy Palestine and kill women and children indiscriminately. Apostate regimes in many countries have become American puppets, joining in the oppression of true Muslims. America also is the leading source of Western corruption that threatens Muslim souls.

The answer and the antidote to these developments is Jihad—Jihad defined as armed struggle.

The United States thus presents both a threat and an opportunity for the Jihadists. While it is hostile to Islam, it provides a common enemy and thereby a basis for building unity among Islam's diverse national, ethnic, and tribal groups.

By taking action, Jihad will awaken the Muslim community, demonstrate the power of Jihad, inspire the faithful, and bring about spiritual revival. Jihad offers an opportunity for revenge, a counter to humiliation. It is a powerful message whose appeal thrives on the failure of ideologies of Arab Socialism, Pan-Arabism, and Ba'athism to bring Arabs and Muslims respect and influence. Jihad feeds on anger.

The Jihadists define themselves and their struggle through action. Islam is to be defended through action. Believers will be galvanized through action. They will be awakened, inspired, and instructed through action. Action will propagate Jihadist ideology, expand the following, and encourage recruitment. Islam's global struggle will be unified through action. Embracing action will shield believers from corruption from the West.

Jihadist strategy is notional and opportunistic. The objectives are broad—to drive out the infidels from Muslim lands, topple "apostate regimes" like the House of Saud and the Egyptian government, foster religious revival, expand the Islamic community, and ultimately reestablish the Caliphate, which, at its height 600 years ago, stretched from the Himalayas to the Pyrenees. But the goal is building a following, not taking ground. The time horizon for success is distant and in any event determined by Allah. Jihadist strategy is neither linear nor sequential. There is no "road map" to victory. Strategic objectives do not dictate action; action is the objective.

As a consequence, continuing operations are imperative. Contributors will not support an inactive organization. Without action as a recruiting poster, potential recruits will go elsewhere. And operations with specific signature (such as simultaneous attacks) ensure "branding"—making clear which organization is in the vanguard. In this, al Qaeda differs little from other revolutionary vanguards in history.

The Jihadists' operational code of warfare emphasizes process and prowess—not progress. Warfare is not a terrible phenomenon, and peace is not the natural state of society. To the contrary, war is a perpetual condition. Man is inherently a warrior, and if not fighting an external foe, men will fight among themselves. Confronting an outside enemy will bring unity and unleash the great strength latent in the Islamic community.

Drawing upon the experiences of warfare in the Arabian peninsula long before the Koran and during centuries of tribal warfare since, Jihadist tactics call for isolated raids, not sustained large-scale operations or long military campaigns. The idea is to lie in wait, attack the enemy when he is inattentive, beleaguer him, make his life untenable. Showmanship in carrying out attacks demonstrates prowess.

For the Jihadist, fighting is a religious obligation. Strength in battle comes from religious conviction, not weapons. Combat is an opportunity to demonstrate one's belief through courage and sacrifice. Heroism is more important than the outcome. Those who sacrifice all are not only to be extolled but will be rewarded in Paradise. Fighting benefits the Jihadist individually and morally.

Of course, none of this means that there are not debates among Jihadists. There are differences:

- Should they concentrate on local conflict or join up with al Qaeda?

- Should they lie low to rebuild?

- Was it wise to launch a terrorist campaign in Saudi Arabia?

- How acceptable are collateral Muslim casualties?

- Should the heretical Shia be enlisted or attacked?

- Are kidnappings, or taking children hostage as in Russia, counterproductive?

To build an Army of Believers, Jihadists consider recruiting as an end in itself, not simply to serve operational needs. Recruiting is decentralized and continuous in an effort to spread Jihadist ideology. The themes emphasized in recruiting efforts are the suffering of the devout, the atrocities committed against Muslims, the injustice of the situation in Muslim communities, the humiliation inflicted on the faithful. Recruiting stresses the opportunities to take action against these wrongs. And Jihadist recruitment offers spiritual rewards.

Recruitment is a multistage self-presentation process in which volunteers must demonstrate increasing commitment to the Jihadist cause. This commitment leads the recruit through successive oaths and into the secret inner circles. Since the end of al Qaeda's sanctuary in Afghanistan, the constant talent hunt for volunteers with specialized skills has been decentralized.

Reconnaissance of targets and planning to carry out attacks are also continuous activities. Planning itself is considered a way to participate in Jihad. Plans are surrogate operations reflecting the planners' ambitions and fantasies. It is based on manuals, playbooks, and observed tactical lessons. At the same time, it is entrepreneurial, offering the opportunity for the Jihadist to take the initiative. Previous operations are examined in order to perfect techniques and to surpass predecessors.

Jihadists also take note of concerns voiced by the public in target countries. For example, public statements that the population is vulnerable to biological or chemical attack are picked up by Jihadists and possibly incorporated into operational planning. These steps are often then confirmed by Western intelligence. Our concerns become self-fulfilling prophecies.

How do things look to the Jihadists three years after 9/11? Any al Qaeda member briefing bin Laden would have to acknowledge that it has been a difficult 36 months since 9/11. The training camps in Afghanistan were dismantled. Thousands of Jihadists have been arrested worldwide. Some of al Qaeda's top planners—talent hard to replace—have been killed or captured. The organization's cash flow has been squeezed.

Moreover, infidels occupy Afghanistan, Saudi Arabia, Kuwait, Iraq, Bahrain, the Emirates, Qatar, and Oman. They threaten Syria. Apostate regimes in Jordan, Palestine, and Southeast Asia assist the infidels. American puppets in Kabul and Islamabad hunt Jihadists with mercenary tribesmen. Muslims are persecuted everywhere, but—apart from the Palestinians—there are no uprisings.

A briefer in Waziristan also would have to note that al Qaeda's communications have been disrupted. The operational environment is difficult. Transactions are dangerous. The organization has been forced to decentralize and risks loss of unity and fragmentation. Everyone in al Qaeda faces the threat of capture or martyrdom.

But, nonetheless, an al Qaeda briefer might also likely conclude that the Jihadists are succeeding. They have survived the infidels' mightiest blows. Recruits continue to join up (though caution is called for about possible infiltrators). America's arrogance has angered Muslims and alienated its allies. The shadow of 9/11 still hangs over the American economy.

Much of the original leadership of al Qaeda remains intact and can communicate publicly as well as clandestinely. A large cadre of loyal dispersed Afghan veterans is sufficient for hundreds of operations. And adequate financing exists to conduct such operations. Not only do preparations for further operations continue, but the pace of operations has accelerated over the last 36 months. Above all, the briefer would conclude that the Jihadists have demonstrated their faith, their courage, their prowess, which will protect their souls, inspire the Muslim world, and show their worthiness before God.

Finally, Osama bin Laden's briefer probably would see America's invasion of Iraq as a gift to the Jihadists. It has split the infidels and provoked the Muslim community. Their so-called quick victory has put American soldiers into a situation where they are vulnerable to the kind of warfare natural to Jihad. Iraq opens a new front for Jihad, one that provides a new, radicalizing experience for hundreds of new recruits. It will provide a new cohort of blooded veterans.

How long can the Americans stay in Iraq? Jihadists note that it took a decade to convince the Soviet Union to leave Afghanistan; they are convinced that America has less spine and little stomach for losses. They question whether the United States could last in Iraq until 2013. And when the Americans depart, chaos will ensue in Iraq, giving Jihad new space to operate. The apostate regimes in the region will, they believe, tremble and fall. With the oil wealth of the region in their hands, they will be able to force the West to abandon Israel, and the Holy Land again will be theirs.

Jihadist visions of the future may include one in which war continues until Judgment Day; continuous terrorist spectaculars inspire a global intifada; Afghanistan, Pakistan, and

Saudi Arabia fall; America suffers a humiliating defeat in Iraq; somehow, someday another 9/11. Perhaps Jihadist beliefs will transcend Islam to become a pervasive anti-U.S. ideology.

The Jihadists believe that in the long run, demographics and economics are on their side with millions of discontented youths in the region and in immigrant communities with no prospects—and many more educated with better economic futures but still seeking spiritual fulfillment, making them a fertile pool for recruitment. They believe that politics are with them; the infidel and apostate tyrants inevitably will fall. The Jihadists are convinced that they are the ones who will replace them.

Brian Michael Jenkins, *Senior Advisor to the President at the RAND Corporation, is one of the world's leading authorities on terrorism and sophisticated crime. He works with government agencies, international organizations, and multinational corporations. From 1989 to 1998, Mr. Jenkins was the deputy chairman of Kroll Associates, an international investigative and consulting firm. Before that, he was chairman of the Political Science Department at RAND where, from 1972 to 1989, he also directed RAND's research on political violence.*

Commissioned in the infantry at the age of 19, Mr. Jenkins became a paratrooper and ultimately a captain in the Green Berets. He is a decorated combat veteran, having served in the Seventh Special Forces Group in the Dominican Republic during the American intervention and, later, as a member of the Fifth Special Forces Group in Vietnam (1966–1967). He returned to Vietnam on a special assignment in 1968 to serve as a civilian member of the Long Range Planning Task Group; he remained with the Group until the end of 1969 and received the Department of the Army's highest award for his service. Mr. Jenkins returned to Vietnam on special assignment in 1971.

In 1996, President Clinton appointed Mr. Jenkins to the White House Commission on Aviation Safety and Security. From 1999 to 2000, he served as an advisor to the National Commission on Terrorism, and in 2000 he was appointed to the U.S. Comptroller General's Advisory Board. He is currently serving his second term on that advisory board. Mr. Jenkins is a research associate at the Mineta Transportation Institute and since 1997 has directed its continuing research on protecting surface transportation against terrorist attacks.

Mr. Jenkins also serves as a special advisor to the International Chamber of Commerce (ICC) and a member of the board of directors of the ICC's Commercial Crime Services. Over the years, Mr. Jenkins also has served as a consultant to or carried out assignments for a number of government agencies.

Mr. Jenkins is the author of International Terrorism: A New Mode of Conflict, *as well as two recent RAND reports on al Qaeda*—Deterrence and Influence in Counterterrorism: A Component in the War on al Qaeda *and* Countering al Qaeda: An Appreciation of the Situation and Suggestions for Strategy. *He is also the editor and coauthor of* Terrorism and Personal Protection, *coeditor and coauthor of* Aviation Terrorism and Security, *and a coauthor of* The Fall of South Vietnam.

Mr. Jenkins has a B.A. in fine arts and an M.A. in history, both from UCLA. He studied at the University of Guanajuato in Mexico and in the Department of Humanities at the University of San Carlos in Guatemala, where he was a Fulbright Fellow and recipient of a second fellowship from the Organization of American States.

CHAPTER THREE

Defeating the Global Jihadist Movement: Results of a RAND Exercise
A Panel Presentation

John Parachini, Moderator
Peter Wilson
David Aaron

John Parachini

The purpose of the RAND exercise was twofold. First, as Brian Jenkins had explained, it is crucial to understand the Jihadist perspective—their goals and the focus of their operations. Second, using these insights, we wanted to assess how well the *National Strategy for Combating Terrorism* counters the next phase of the global Jihadist movement. This exercise constitutes an exploratory approach, not a predictive one. Exercises and scenarios like this help gain insight into gaps in our understanding and gaps in our preparation, and identify new ways to grapple with the problem.

The exercise was tested once inside RAND, and then outside participants were called upon for a second iteration. These participants consisted of experts on the Middle East and South Asia, and counterterrorism and former government officials from the Clinton and Bush administrations. This presentation focuses for the most part on this second exercise.

The Exercise Methodology
First, the participants were briefed on how the game would be played, and then Brian Jenkins gave them a version of the presentation you just saw, to get them into a Jihadist frame of mind. Second, the participants were divided into two groups. Each of them debated among themselves about the strategy and objectives the movement should now pursue as if they were to present their conclusions to the top Jihadist leadership.

This was followed by a joint meeting of the two groups to present their conclusions to one another. Next, the two groups divided up again, each holding a mock National Security Council meeting to assess the current *National Strategy for Combating Terrorism*. Finally, the groups met together again in a plenary session to present the conclusion of their deliberations.

The exercise demonstrated that it was difficult to simulate the command structure of a global, religiously motivated Jihadist movement. The biggest challenge in an exercise of this nature is not "group-think" but "culture-think"—where one's cultural biases and outlook must be overcome to play a role of a very alien nature.

Peter Wilson

The present *National Strategy for Combating Terrorism* describes the threat, its scope, and inter-linkages in the following chart.

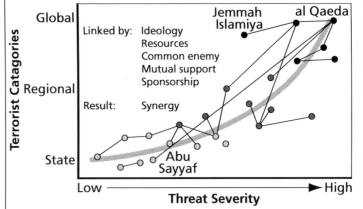

RAND *CF212-1*

U.S. Government Strategy and Assessment of the Problem

The objectives set forth in *National Strategy for Combating Terrorism* are fourfold:

(1) Defeat terrorists and their organizations. The operational goal is to identify terrorist organizations and individuals, locate them, and destroy them.

(2) Deny sponsorship, support, and sanctuary to terrorists; end the state sponsorship of terrorism; establish and maintain an international standard of accountability for terrorist actions; undertake efforts to strengthen and sustain the international effort to fight terrorism; conduct operations to interdict and disrupt material support for terrorists; and finally, eliminate terrorist sanctuaries and havens.

(3) Diminish the underlying conditions that terrorists seek to exploit. Partner with the international community to strengthen weak states and prevent the emergence or reemergence of terrorism. Win the war of ideas.

(4) Defend U.S. citizens and interests at home and abroad. Implement the *National Strategy for Homeland Security*. Enhance measures to ensure the integrity, reliability, and availability of critical physical and information-based infrastructures at home and abroad. Ensure an integrated incident management capability. Integrate into our programs measures to protect U.S. citizens abroad.

The ultimate goal of these efforts is not to eradicate terrorism but to return terrorism to the "criminal domain." This is represented graphically in the following chart.

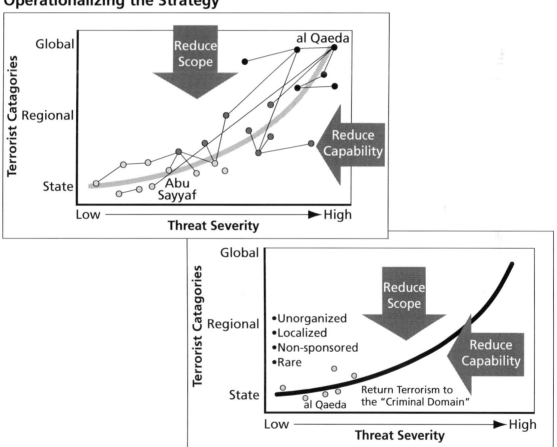

RAND *CF212-2*

Returning Terrorism to the Criminal Domain

Taking these goals and operational objectives into account, the Jihadist portion of the exercise revealed several differences on key questions. Was al Qaeda a centralized organization in decline, or a decentralized and adaptive movement posing new challenges? From the Jihadist viewpoint, should al Qaeda seek a single sanctuary that would be vulnerable to attack, or encourage a decentralized approach to Jihad movement that would risk command and control? Participants cited Pakistan as a possible target for the first approach because of its political instability and nuclear weapons capability. The attacks in Bali, Mombasa, Casablanca, and Madrid were cited as examples of the second approach.

The consensus was that attacking U.S. global influence remains a central goal of the Jihadist movement. But there was debate as to whether the United States is a near-term targeting priority and, if it were, whether the goal should be one "terrorist spectacular" exceeding 9/11 violence or several small attacks at such places as subways, sports events, or shopping malls?

There were also two views on the significance of Iraq as a strategic focus for the Jihadists. Should they take advantage of Iraqi insurgency, or was it proceeding well on its own? Alternatively, should they focus on other valuable targets in an effort to "broaden the front"? Interestingly, there was a conspicuous lack of focus by the groups on operations to affect the U.S. election, nor was there much discussion of using CBRN [chemical, biological, radiological, or nuclear] weapons. Moreover, there was no consideration of Israel as a target for the Jihadists.

As for the *National Strategy for Combating Terrorism*, one of the groups believed the strategy as expressed in the February 2003 document was adequate, while the other group thought that major revisions were needed.

However, both groups agreed that there has not been enough effort on the "diminish" component of the current strategy, i.e., "diminish the underlying conditions that terrorists seek to exploit." Specifically, it was essential to develop an effective U.S. message and articulate it in a constructive lexicon that will appeal to Muslims. It is critical to wage a war of ideas in the Islamic world and develop regional voices of moderation.

Finally, there was a strong consensus that a better definition of the threat is critically needed. Are we waging a war on terrorism or a struggle against global Jihadism? Several participants called for a new national estimate on the threat.

David Aaron

The origins of the exercise lay in the recognition that most threat assessments are in fact vulnerability or feasibility assessments. They look at our weaknesses and the technical capability of terrorists to carry out specific attacks. In contrast, we sought insights—not what Jihadists *could* do, but what they *would* do. We also wanted to get at the interaction of strategies, theirs versus ours. To do that, we needed to play out their reactions to our offensive and defensive measures. This would suggest what further steps we might need in response.

Several conclusions could be drawn from both versions of the exercise. First, it is very difficult to get into the mind-set of the Jihadist. While this may seem obvious, it was not the case with "red team" exercises during the Cold War, in which players found it relatively easy to slip into the roles of their adversaries. Despite background papers and briefings (participants even addressed each other as "brother" and "sister"), in the end the participants tended to analyze situations as if they were a secular enemy. This is not an intelligence problem. It is not the result of a lack of data or information. It is a cultural/philosophical problem.

Second, it was equally hard to apply insight that the participants did gain from the exercise to the U.S. strategic approach. There was general agreement that most *elements* of a U.S. strategy are in place, but there is little sense of priority and an inadequate appreciation of the linkages between these elements. Moreover, U.S. strategy is essentially an attrition strategy in a region where 50 percent to 75 percent of the population is under the age of 24—a questionable equation. The *National Strategy* focuses on tactical steps and not enough on genuine strategy. For example, reducing terrorism to a local police matter is inadequate guidance for what must be done. It is not responsive to the long-term struggle inside Islam, which almost everyone saw as a crucial dimension in meeting the terrorist challenge.

How should U.S. strategy be changed? Much more emphasis must be placed on keeping Jihadism from spreading. It is crucial to recognize that we are in an ideological war.

Third, we were unable to get participation from any Arab-Americans in the RAND exercise. Is asking Arab-Americans to play the role of terrorists seen as an insult? Or is the political environment a deterrent? What can be done about it? We need to find a way to take advantage of America's multicultural society.

Finally, a major educational effort is needed if we are going to engage in what has been called a "generational struggle." During the Cold War, the response of universities was to create centers for Soviet and Communist studies. Foundation and federal money was available. Emigrés played a major role in helping Americans understand communism and the Soviet threat. While there are some university Islamic studies programs, no comparable effort is being made today. Perhaps it is because, unlike the Cold War, the war on terror is not seen as an existential struggle. But it could become one. The Jihadists are explicitly calling for a "Clash of Civilizations."

John Parachini *is acting associate director of the Intelligence Policy Center at the RAND Corporation. He has led RAND projects on the propensity of terrorists to acquire chemical, biological, radiological, and nuclear weapons, how the U.S. government can capture digital information terrorists leave around the globe, scenario development for counterterrorism planning, and the danger of terrorists and rogue states acquiring nuclear material expertise from the former Soviet Union. Mr. Parachini is editing a volume of case studies on the propensity of terrorists to acquire nuclear, biological, and chemical weapons. He has testified before both houses of Congress and published articles on terrorism and weapons proliferation in the* Washington Quarterly, Arms Control Today, RAND Review, The Nonproliferation Review, Studies in Conflict & Terrorism, *the* Los Angeles Times, *the* San Francisco Chronicle, Newsday, *and the* International Herald Tribune.

Previously he served as the executive director of the Washington office of the Monterey Institute of International Studies' Center for Nonproliferation Studies.

Mr. Parachini holds a B.A. in philosophy from Haverford College, an M.A. in international relations from the Johns Hopkins University Nitze School of Advanced International Studies, and an M.B.A. from Georgetown University.

Peter Wilson *is a senior political scientist at the RAND Corporation who specializes in defense policy and planning research. To that end, he is the coauthor of the RAND "Day After" strategic planning exercise methodology that has been used to explore major national security issues such as developing counter-proliferation investment strategies, dealing with adaptive (asymmetric) threats, and developing information operations plans and policies. He was the co–principal investigator of a study for NASA looking into options to "competitively source" and/or privatize the Space Shuttle program.*

Mr. Wilson has also coauthored a number of major studies for the Department of Defense on the implications of the changing global security environment on U.S. defense planning and investment. In addition to coauthoring a variety of major RAND studies, he has written essays on a wide range of national security issues for the Institute for National Strategic Studies Strategic Assessment series, the Strategic Studies Institute of the U.S. Army War College, the Washington Quarterly, *the Progressive Policy Institute, and* Parameters. *His most recent publication is "An Alternative Future Force: Building a Better Army," with John Gordon IV and David E. Johnson (*Parameters, *Winter 2003–04).*

Mr. Wilson holds a B.A. in political science from Princeton University and an M.A. in political science from the University of Chicago.

Ambassador David Aaron *has served in both the government and the private sector. A graduate of Occidental College and Princeton University, Ambassador Aaron entered the Foreign Service in 1962, where he held a variety of posts, which included the U.S. Delegation to NATO and to the Strategic Arms Limitation Talks with the Soviet Union. After leaving the Foreign Service, he continued in government in several positions, including the National Security Council, Task Force Director for the Senate Intelligence Committee, and then Deputy National Security Advisor to President Jimmy Carter. In the latter capacity, he also served as a confidential presidential emissary to Europe, the Middle East, Africa, Latin America, and China.*

Upon leaving government, Ambassador Aaron became Vice President for Mergers and Acquisitions at Oppenheimer & Co. and vice chairman of the board of Oppenheimer International.

During the Clinton administration, he served as ambassador to the Organization for Economic Cooperation and Development (OECD) in Paris. At the same time, he was appointed Special White House Envoy for Cryptography, to develop international guidelines for encryption technology in trade and communications. Subsequently, Ambassador Aaron was appointed Undersecretary of Commerce for International Trade.

After leaving government in 2000, he became Senior International Advisor to the law firm Dorsey LLP. In the fall of 2003, he was appointed senior fellow and Assistant to the President for Research on Counterterrorism at the RAND Corporation.

CHAPTER FOUR

Democracy and Islam: The Struggle in the Islamic World
A Strategy for the United States

Cheryl Benard

After 9/11, defining the opponent is the first challenge. Are we engaged in a "war on terror"? Or is the opponent a radical ideology that misrepresents true Islam while acting in its name? Or is radical Islam—a fringe element within the overall religion—the problem?

As President George W. Bush said on August 6, 2004, "We actually misnamed the war on terror. It ought to be called the struggle against ideological extremists who do not believe in free societies, and who happen to use terror as a weapon." Islam is engaged in a monumental struggle over values, identity, and its place in the world. It is grappling with fundamental questions. What kind of society does Islam require its followers to live in? How should such a society be brought about? Who speaks for Islam? What should the relations with the non-Islamic world look like?

U.S. goals in this struggle include preventing the spread of extremism and violence; assessing which groups are violent and dangerous; encouraging trends that will foster development, prosperity, stability, and social progress; and identifying the right partners and priorities for our policies.

The United States tends to view the Islamic world as bipolar, as radicals vs. conservatives. U.S. policy is focused on radical and destructive elements as the "problem" and moderate elements as the "solution." But this concept of Islam is too generic; it does not do justice to the complexity and dynamism of the situation. As a result, we are failing to support important trends and incorrectly identifying who are our best partners.

Understanding this debate becomes easier if we realize that the answers to the most controversial questions within Islam include a range of views. Think of these views as falling along a spectrum. Looking at where different Islamic groups and individuals stand on certain critical "marker issues" is a way of placing them on that spectrum. It is then possible to determine which segments of the spectrum are compatible with our values and which are inimical. Other things being equal, we would naturally prefer the former to the latter, and cooperation with groups who oppose our basic values should only happen under exceptional circumstances when unavoidable for tactical reasons. Correctly identifying the differing Islamic ideological postures will allow us to find ways to support suitable partners and positive trends and to begin to outline a strategy for tailored responses to the current conflict within Islam.

Certain "marker issues" help locate Islamic groups ideologically. The most reliable are

- democracy, human rights
- Shari'a law vs. civil law
- rights of minorities
- status of women
- legal rights
- public participation
- segregation
- "lifestyle" issues.

Less reliable marker issues are attitudes toward violence, and elections—because there is a temptation for groups to dissimulate and to misrepresent their actual views on those issues in order to avoid repercussions.

The ideological spectrum for contemporary Islamic views produced by these marker issues is indicated below:

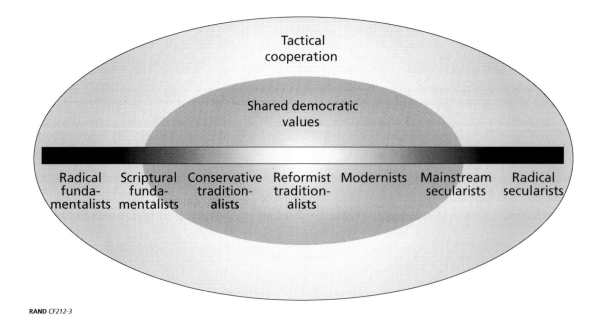

RAND CF212-3

Ideological Spectrum for Contemporary Islamic Views

These groups have the following characteristics: Radical fundamentalists want an authoritarian, puritanical state in which prescribed behavior is imposed by force. They see violence and terrorism as appropriate methods for achieving their goals. Moreover, they take great liberties in defining their version of what is Islamic. They are seldom careful students of Islamic orthodoxy and instead feel free to invent and interpret. Examples of such radical fundamentalists are the Taliban, al Qaeda, and the Islamic Movement of Uzbekistan.

The scriptural fundamentalists also believe in an Islamic state where correct behavior is coercively imposed. They are prepared to accept Islamic democracy, but not Western democracy. These scriptural fundamentalists try to base policies on a study of orthodox Islamic texts and include in their ranks actual Islamic scholars. Violence is acceptable to them, but they prefer to exempt civilians and fellow Muslims. An example would be the ruling elites in the Islamic Republic of Iran.

Conservative traditionalists prefer an Islamic state, but have learned to "live with" many different kinds of governments. They carve out their niche in Muslim communities, where they seek to influence daily life and behavior. Believing in Shari'a law, they would like to see it implemented wherever possible. An example is the Northern States of Nigeria. While they do not preach violence, they are socially backward-looking, hold values incompatible with development, and sympathize with fundamentalists. At times they support them and provide "institutional cover."

Reformist traditionalists think some accommodation should be made to history and to changing social conditions. They believe that Shari'a has often been misinterpreted or applied too repressively and can be moderated and adapted to the modern age. To them, an Islamic state is less important than a vibrant, attractive Islam.

The problem with this group as a partner is that they are often very engrossed in apologetics, in elaborate examinations of texts and insider debates. They are cautious and slow to move, and are not very attractive to young people and to activists. An example is King Zaher Shah and the Afghan monarchists.

The modernists believe that Islam is compatible with democracy, human rights, modern life, and individual freedom. In their view, Islam is subject to history and change. The original Koranic rules are not literally eternal. It is the principles that should be upheld, not the details. In essence, they think Islam needs a "Protestant Reformation."

The problem with considering them as partners is that, in the West, they don't have much funding, get little publicity, and tend to be academic, and in the Islamic world, they are often persecuted and jailed. A good example is Professor Aghajari, an Iranian dissident who received a death sentence (since suspended) for saying that Muslims should think for themselves and not be blindly obedient to clerics.

The mainstream secularists believe in the separation of church and state. They see Islam as a private individual practice that should not contravene human rights and civil law. Practices in conflict with that (e.g., hudud criminal punishments such as flogging and stoning) are no longer acceptable. Unfortunately, the mainstream secularists today lack ideological and political support. An historical example would be Ataturk.

Radical secularists are affiliated with leftist, socialist, or communist ideologies or movements, and other totalitarian/autocratic political philosophies. They believe in separation of church and state, and social justice. However, they are often anti-American, accept use of violence and at times terrorism, and can be strongly antidemocratic. One example is the Popular Front for the Liberation of Palestine (PFLP).

The basic elements of a U.S. strategy to deal with the struggle within Islam would

- support the modernists first
- support the traditionalists to keep them viable against radical fundamentalists
- oppose fundamentalists energetically
- support secularists where appropriate
- strengthen civil society.

To level the playing field, it is critical to give modernists more resources. Modernism is what worked for the West. We should be prepared to subsidize the publication of their work in a variety of forms such as the Web, textbooks, pamphlets, and conferences. We should encourage them to address their work to mass audiences and help distribute their work widely. We should popularize modernists as role models and leaders, and provide venues and platforms to communicate their message.

Support for secularists when appropriate also needs to be part of our approach. Mainstream secularists, while still a minority in the Islamic world, may be growing. This possibility should neither be overlooked nor inadvertently stifled. In particular, a secular-based civil society is alive and trying to emerge throughout the Islamic world (nongovernmental organizations [NGOs] dealing with environmental issues, youth issues, and women's affairs are booming in Iran, and, elsewhere, civic associations devoted to culture and sports are very active). In the Islamic world, the religious lens is not the only view available. Above all, secularists need and deserve support on crucial issues of civil liberties, human rights, and social advancement.

The temptation is for Western policymakers to identify the traditionalists as the main partners for outreach to the Muslim world. Because they are overtly and visibly "Islamic," it is obvious evidence that one is "reaching out" to Muslims. Moreover, they have structures, leaders, institutions, publications, and events that can easily be found. And finally, some are willing to openly renounce violence, take moderate positions, and accept the principle of dialogue with other faiths and the West.

It is appropriate to selectively support the traditionalists. Though they are not the optimal partners, they can be important in certain circumstances. Traditionalists can prevent radicals from forcing a fabricated, eccentric version of Islam on uneducated populations (e.g., Taliban vs. the much more tolerant and moderate Afghan traditional Islam). Through their local legitimacy and influence, they can safeguard public opinion against extremist inroads. We should provide education and training in communication skills, and access to public opinion where needed.

However, in many respects they are unsuitable partners. They are not good partners in the task of development: Decades of poverty and educational and social decline in the Muslim world took place on their watch. They can be close to fundamentalists ideologically and practically and often say different things to different audiences. They represent only a small minority among expatriates. They hold backward views—with which a partner can unwittingly become associated. They have little appeal to young people or activists. Supporting them weakens the modernists.

It is also necessary to aggressively confront fundamentalists on more than just terrorism. We should help expose inaccuracies in their interpretation of Islam. We need to more broadly publicize the human costs of their violent acts. We should help dramatize their inability to govern to the benefit of their societies. For example, in Iran the economy is in a shambles and crime is up despite implementation of Shari'a law. This should be made public in locations such as Pakistan or Nigeria, where fundamentalists are arguing that Shari'a law must be implemented to combat crime. Ways need to be found to encourage investigative journalists to explore issues of corruption, immorality, and hypocrisy in fundamentalist and terrorist circles.

Would U.S. support be the "kiss of death" for our potential friends? This varies by the setting. It can be dangerous in some situations, but we should not overlook that it can be a positive thing as well. It is important to note that "partner" is not the same as "tool." And in the end, resources can outweigh negative associations. Moreover, it is not so much a matter of taking sides or intervening as it is a matter of leveling the playing field. We should not forget that U.S. values are still widely admired in the Muslim world.

Disregarding compatibility of values can lead to catastrophic policy errors. Working with extremists in the Afghan war with the USSR helped fuel radical fundamentalism in Afghanistan and Pakistan. Fear of Shia radicalism in Iran caused us to tolerate the growth of Wahhabi influence elsewhere. We thereby inadvertently assisted the emergence and growth of the Taliban and al Qaeda. History shows that being too tactical without enough forethought is risky. We may have an agenda—but so does the other side. It behooves us to be very certain that we know what it is, lest we unknowingly advance it to our detriment.

To sum up: U.S. policy tends to focus only on the fundamentalists and the traditionalists; the distinctions among fundamentalists are important and should not be ignored; the traditionalists have merits but should not be idealized as the real Islam; change is happening, and U.S. engagement can have the greatest positive influence in regard to those points on the ideological spectrum that we are overlooking.

What has been the reaction to this study? In reviewing it, a radical fundamentalist writer and known supporter of bin Laden said:

> This is a political strategic paper for the White House Administration in order to face Islamic fundamentalism. Whoever reads this paper will find that it is a very dangerous and important paper.

—Abdullah Al-Nafisi
Secretary General
Popular Convention for
Anti-Normalization with the Zionist Entity
Al Jazeera, 23 June 2004

Cheryl Benard *is a senior political scientist and director of the Initiative for Middle Eastern Youth (IMEY) at the RAND Corporation. Her research interests include refugee and immigrant integration; gender in development; issues in the delivery of humanitarian crisis relief; education reform; radicalization and youth; and post-conflict nation-building. Since writing her dissertation on Arab nationalism, Islam and the Middle East have been strong themes in her work. Her study of the Iranian revolution was entitled* The Government of God *(Columbia University Press, 1984). Dr. Benard's most recent books are* Veiled Courage *(Random House, 2002), which* *describes civil resistance against the Taliban, and* Civil Democratic Islam *(RAND, 2003), which suggests a way to better understand Islamic political groups and movements by aligning them along a differentiated ideological spectrum. In addition to her research, she has developed curricula and conducted training programs for peacekeepers, police, and the military.*

Dr. Benard holds a B.A. in political science from the American University of Beirut, Lebanon, and a Ph.D. in international relations from the University of Vienna, Austria.

CHAPTER FIVE

Defending America Against Suicide Terrorism

Bruce Hoffman

Over the last few years, suicide terrorism has grown in frequency. In the 1970s, it hardly existed. In the 1990s, the average number of suicide attacks worldwide averaged 2.5 per year. Starting in 2001, the number of suicide attacks leapt to 41, then 45 in 2002, and 57 in 2003. Within the first quarter of 2004, there were more than 100 suicide attacks.

Moreover, these attacks have grown in lethality. While there were spikes in the numbers of fatalities over the years (in 1998 about 300 people were killed), the totals from 2001 to this year are climbing dramatically. Excluding 9/11, for 2001, there were 188 deaths. In 2002, there were 384; 2003 saw 628 fatalities from suicide attacks. Within the first quarter of 2004, the number of fatalities from suicide attacks has exceeded 1,100—and none of these numbers include fatalities in Iraq.

It seems very likely that we will see more suicide attacks in the United States in the future. The suicide aspect of the 9/11 attacks was essential to their success and stunning impact. Even before 9/11, suicide attacks were either contemplated (Oklahoma City bomber Timothy McVeigh, who found another way) or planned but disrupted. In 2000, two Palestinians plotted suicide bombings in the New York subway, but an informant's tip allowed police to foil the plot less than a day away from the attack. And of course, suicide attacks have long been conducted against Americans abroad.

Based on global patterns, three types of suicide attacks would most likely occur in the United States. The first would involve mass casualties and high-value, symbolic targets such as buildings or installations (e.g., the White House, the U.S. Capitol building, the Pentagon, or other federal office buildings). Another such target would be a major means of conveyance (e.g., the George Washington Bridge, the Golden Gate Bridge, the Holland Tunnel).

The second type of suicide attack would aim at high-value, symbolic targets against specific persons. The president, cabinet members, Supreme Court justices, senators and congressmen, mayors—all could be marked for political assassinations.

Third, suicide terrorists could deliberately conduct lethal attacks against the public. This would include bus, train, and subway bombings, and attacks on shopping malls, cinemas, sports stadiums, and pedestrian malls. To address the issue of how the United States should deal with the prospect of such attacks, it is necessary to answer three questions:

- Why is suicide bombing so attractive to terrorists?
- How can the United States defend against suicide attacks?
- How can the United States mitigate the damage caused by a suicide attack?

To answer these questions, we conducted extensive research and interviews with foreign police/security forces with prior experience with suicide terrorism. The following conclusions emerged.

First, from a tactical standpoint, suicide attacks are attractive to terrorists because they are inexpensive and effective—with an extremely favorable per-casualty cost benefit for the terrorists. Moreover, they are less complicated and compromising than other lethal operations. No escape plan is needed because, if successful, there will be no assailant to capture and interrogate. Suicide attacks are perhaps the ultimate "smart bombs." They can cleverly employ disguise and deception and effect last-minute changes in timing, access, and choice of target. Finally, suicide attacks guarantee media coverage. They offer the irresistible combination of savagery and bloodshed.

Second, social and individual incentives also make suicide attacks attractive. For Muslims, there is a perceived religious justification for the act. This comes from both the organizations responsible for attacks and the communities from which terrorists are recruited. Suicide attackers do not make a distinction between that and martyrdom.

There are also religious incentives to both would-be bombers and to their families. Perhaps even more important than the proverbial 72 virgins waiting in paradise for Muslim male bombers is the claim that female as well as male martyrs will ensure a place in heaven for 70 relatives—regardless of their piety or sins. Lastly, in addition to the spiritual considerations, there is material encouragement in the form of financial payments made to bombers' families: The surviving family is provided nicer living accommodations and a wealth of consumer goods.

How can the United States defend against suicide attacks? We must change both our mind-set and our approach.

For example, simple profiling of suicide bombers is no longer effective. Suicide attackers can be young or old, male or female, religious or secular. Equipment is becoming more sophisticated. Bombers now use less obtrusive belt bombs.

The best defense relies on mobilizing the entire security force against the threat of suicide terrorism. It is not sufficient to rely on highly trained, elite specialized units. A countersuicide mind-set must be instilled in each and every policeman. All security forces must be briefed, involved in the mission, and made thoroughly aware of the threat. They must understand the permutations of possible attacks, the various indicators, the most effective responses, and the details of plans to counter such attacks.

As it turns out, a highly visible security presence is effective against suicide terrorists. Interrogations with failed bombers reveal that a large police presence around potential targets can disrupt attacks. A covert presence is essential, but visible, static, and mobile security deployments are also key. Deterrence must be made highly visible throughout the potential target area.

Police must also assume a "hunter" rather than "fisherman" mind-set. They need to actively seek out, observe, and track their "prey." To counter an attack, both intelligence (e.g., advance warning) and knowledge management are critical. The communication system must provide information and knowledge to officers on the street so they can act instantly should the time arise.

How can the United States mitigate the damage caused by a suicide attack? The answer is to treat the attack as both a medical emergency and a criminal investigation.

An immediate response is critical, but can risk more serious problems. Doctors in Israel, for instance, have found that 90 percent of those who die in suicide attacks are killed immediately, but many of the other 10 percent can be saved. The wounded must receive medical attention within 10 minutes, be quickly stabilized, and then moved to a hospital immediately. But haste provides opportunity for a second, more devastating attack, killing valuable EMS [Emergency Medical Services] personnel as well.

Thus, law enforcement and other first responders must synchronize their responses. Security personnel have to immediately cordon off the scene and push back the crowd. Next, they must quickly search for possible secondary explosive devices or bombers. Only then should they grant access to the emergency crews.

A criminal investigation also must be part of the immediate and ongoing response. Plans should be made to quickly dispatch mobile police forces patrolling the area and to send additional forces to the scene. They can help cordon off the site, control crowds, and/or identify witnesses. The latter must be done quickly, and witnesses removed from scene for questioning. This is important not only to be able reconstruct details of the attack but also to identify possible logistical support or guidance from others at the scene. At the same time, it is necessary to intensify countersurveillance around likely targets in advance of any potential attack.

All law enforcement/security personnel should be trained to be aware of people surveilling the attack site. Identified persons should be stopped and questioned with the details recorded in a database. This can be used to match against prior reports of surveillance, which can help find the "handlers" of the suicide terrorist.

In conclusion, it is critical to recognize that we are neither powerless nor defenseless against this threat. We need to avoid falling prey to the psychological paralysis that terrorists intend to create with this tactic. There are concrete things we can do to defend against and mitigate such attacks. For example, Israel cites a 30 percent decrease in number of Palestinian attacks—including suicide attacks—from 2002 to 2003 with a 50 percent decrease in the number of casualties.

Defending against and mitigating attacks requires that we change our mind-set and approach to suicide terrorism. We must begin to meet that challenge now.

Bruce Hoffman, *one of the world's leading experts on terrorism, is director of the RAND Corporation's Washington Office and acting director of the RAND Center for Middle East Public Policy. Dr. Hoffman has been at the forefront of RAND's terrorism research for more than two decades. From 2001 to 2004, he served as RAND's Vice President for External Affairs. During the spring of 2004, he was Senior Adviser on Counterterrorism to the Office of National Security Affairs, Coalition Provisional Authority (CPA) in Baghdad. Dr. Hoffman is a senior fellow at the*

Combating Terrorism Center, U.S. Military Academy, West Point, New York, and an adjunct professor in the Security Studies Program at Georgetown University, Washington, D.C.

Dr. Hoffman was the founding director of the Centre for the Study of Terrorism and Political Violence at the University of St Andrews in Scotland, where he was also Reader in International Relations and chairman of the Department of International Relations. In 1994, the Director of Central Intelligence awarded Dr. Hoffman the United States Intelligence Community Seal Medallion, the highest level of commendation given to a nongovernment employee.

In recognition of his academic contributions to the study of political violence, Dr. Hoffman was awarded in June 1998 the first Santiago Grisolía Prize and accompanying Chair in Violence Studies by the Queen Sofía Center for the Study of Violence in Valencia, Spain.

He is editor-in-chief of Studies in Conflict and Terrorism, *the leading scholarly journal in the field, and a member of the advisory board of* Terrorism and Political Violence. *His latest book,* Inside Terrorism, *is published by Columbia University Press in the United States and by Orion Books in Britain. Foreign language editions have been published in nine countries, and it is widely regarded as one of the seminal texts on contemporary terrorism. Dr. Hoffman is also a regular contributor to the* Atlantic Monthly *and was the author of "The Logic of Suicide Terrorism," the cover story of the June 2003 issue.*

Dr. Hoffman holds degrees in government and history, and received his D.Phil. in international relations from Oxford University.

CHAPTER SIX

Terrorism and Intelligence Reform
A Panel Presentation

Lynn Davis, Moderator
Michael Wermuth
Kevin O'Connell
Gregory Treverton

Lynn Davis

Intelligence reform is certainly not a new subject. In fact, going back as far as the late 1940s, we've been debating how to balance the need to coordinate our national intelligence activities while still protecting the perspectives and prerogatives of the various departments and agencies.

What has been particularly surprising is the remarkable consensus that has formed on part of the 9/11 Commission for a radical and unique blueprint for intelligence reform. But then again, no consensus has formed around the proposals themselves, as we have new proposals coming from the White House and again from Congress and from many outside governments. So we still face the issues that we have had all these number of years: how to provide policymakers with analysis that is not biased by the individual perspectives of the departments and agencies, and how to ensure that competing views are introduced into the formulation of intelligence estimates, so as to avoid "the failure of imagination," in the words of the 9/11 Commission, or the "groupthink," in the words of those who looked at our intelligence on weapons of mass destruction in Iraq.

The issues also include how to conduct our intelligence operations while protecting Americans' liberties and ensuring that our intelligence collection meets the operational needs of our departments both for military and covert operations. Now those issues need to be viewed through the prism of how we conduct our war on terrorism. In some ways, this is an even greater challenge: to look across activities, both overseas and domestic, and achieve co-ordination across the foreign and domestic divide.

Our panel members are going to take up that particular task today—to look at terrorism and intelligence reform—each bringing a perspective informed by experiences both within the government and now as analysts here at RAND.

Michael Wermuth

One could argue that there is little new in the 9/11 Commission's recommendations on intelligence. Various forms of their main recommendations—e.g., major reform of the intelligence community, including a Director of National Intelligence and the creation of a National Counterterrorism Center—have been proposed by other commissions or organizations and in legislative initiatives in Congress over many years, but those opportunities passed by.

So why now? Why is there so much attention and urgency to the proposals at this particular point in time, especially since similar proposals have also been made, both before as well as in the aftermath of the 9/11 attacks? Before 9/11, various departments and agencies and their patrons in Congress had been successful in protecting their intelligence prerogatives and in avoiding major reforms. There were arguably no catalytic events to prompt major overhauls.

Moreover, there are significant differences in the operational and actionable intelligence required by military commanders, as opposed to that required by other intelligence community entities. Military commanders require timely information on enemy weapons, tactics, and dispositions. Prior to 9/11, the FBI successfully argued that law enforcement intelligence was not only different but that it needed to be protected for prosecutorial purposes. The various agencies' patrons in Congress have been resilient over the years not only in forestalling significant changes within the executive branch, but also being loathe to clean up its own structures and processes.

Since the 9/11 attacks and the recent Commission recommendations, the legislative vehicles have clearly existed, but there has been very limited interest. I could be cynical and suggest that one main reason is that this is silly season in the nation's capital. It is the summer of an even-numbered year divisible by four. There are clearly sharp political overtones and potentially significant election-year ramifications swirling around the president and Congress on the recommendations that have been made.

Another factor is the somewhat unprecedented media coverage given to the 9/11 Commission proceedings and the release of its report occasioned in no small part by the controversy surrounding the creation of the Commission in the first place, the debate about extending its tenure, and the dramatic charges leveled in front of televised hearings by some very colorful witnesses.

Lastly, Commission members, individually and collectively, are engaged in an intensive lobbying effort with Congress and the public to press for the implementation of their recommendations. The 9/11 Commission also noted Congress's role in the process and recommended some reforms on the Hill. It remains to be seen whether Congress, especially those affected committee chairs and ranking members, will be willing even to acknowledge those points as imperatives, much less take action on the reforms. I'm not optimistic.

But what is missing in all of this, particularly from the 9/11 Commission, is intelligence that is being used and can be collected at the state and local levels, and to some extent by industries in the private sector. Nowhere in its discussion of intelligence reorganization is there any discussion of how these parts fit into an integrated intelligence process. Likewise, the report addresses fundamentally only U.S. intelligence issues and structures. For a global war on terrorism to be truly successful, robust but prudent collaborative intelligence activities with allies, including some very nontraditional ones, is an imperative, especially when faced with a near-global reach of even single organizations like al Qaeda. The Commission makes general hortatory comments but is very short on specifics about international cooperation.

So what lies ahead? We have a plethora of bills that have been introduced in Congress by Pat Roberts and most recently the measure introduced yesterday by Senator John McCain and Senator Joe Lieberman. We have the President's recent executive orders. Recently, a senator likened the current situation to a moving train where Congress is going to be forced to make some decisions. Hopefully they will make the right ones.

Lynn Davis

Thank you, Mike. You've mentioned the sharing of intelligence as key to the war on terrorism, not only within our own government but also with others, and this is exactly what Kevin O'Connell is going to address. Kevin has been an intelligence analyst in the Department of Defense, the State Department, and the White House, as well as for the Director of Central Intelligence.

Kevin O'Connell

The topic of terrorism and intelligence reform has a number of complex dimensions, some of which relate to the broader intelligence mission, but some of which are particularly unique. I want to focus today on intelligence sharing, which we are told is critical to winning the war on terror. However, before I begin, I'd like to raise three more general issues about the context for intelligence on 9/11 with which the audience may not be familiar. Why do I raise them? First, because of their relevance to the war on terror, and second, because if U.S. intelligence is to change, these underlying factors must change as well.

First, the intelligence system on 9/11: collection, analysis, covert action, and counterintelligence were relatively well known by our friends and by our adversaries. Our adversaries know that we collect pictures from space and that we intercept signals, and no longer do terrorists and proliferators hang out on the embassy cocktail circuit. This is something that we have to change.

Second, the intelligence agencies, unlike the way we manage the Department of Defense and our national security apparatus, have both operational and modernization missions embedded in the same agencies. As intelligence grew more complex through the 1990s, with relatively few resources to be brought to bear on the problem, many of the agency heads were forced to mortgage the future to satisfy the day's intelligence mission.

Lastly, the issue of intelligence reform or intelligence transformation is very much in vogue today. Unlike the past when very few people would speak publicly about intelligence, there is today a cacophony of voices that are sometimes well intended, sometimes misinformed, but all of which are talking about intelligence reform. One of the things I fear is that this zeal for reform masks a decade of intelligence reform efforts by people in the intelligence community; it was not on 9/11 that we woke up and recognized we needed to change. During the 1990s, there were more than 16 different commissions with hundreds of recommendations.

What did not exist during that decade was the political consensus that we must change. And if there is a silver lining in the cloud hanging over today's U.S. intelligence community, it is the fact that we do have a political consensus that we need to change.

Rather than simply being a political statement or a general statement of support for reform, I hope this means that we will again allow a robust period of experimentation and innovation, some of which will test political limits and some of which will test limits of technology.

Now let me turn to intelligence sharing specifically. We are told that effective intelligence sharing is something that will help us combat terrorism, and I believe that is absolutely the case. September 11 was in fact an information and intelligence-sharing problem across the government—it was not the first time nor will it be the last time. In fact, what I would describe as one of the biggest myths of 9/11 is that we recognized only then that we had a problem between intelligence and law enforcement. In fact, the record will show that more than a decade's worth of efforts went into attempts to try to bring those two communities closer on how they think about information and how they share information. The recommendations and actions that have taken place since 9/11 have been largely focused on organizational issues such as the creation of the Terrorist Threat Integration Center (TTIC), the Department of Homeland Security, and, of course, the new National Counterterrorism Center.

What are the key issues associated with intelligence sharing? Let me touch on a few of them: bureaucratic rules, cultures, and structures; the role of security; the challenges of analysis; and in particular the issue of how to share publicly. Let's talk about each of those in turn.

Historically, we might characterize "intelligence sharing" as something that took place generally, from us, the United States, to our partners. A one-way flow that was generally outward and that was largely data, not analysis. Relatively little sharing took place across boundaries within the government, although in certain cases the methods by which to share were well established: tear lines on reports which separated information from nonsensitive information and the exchange of technical staff and others.

It is very important that we set the expectations of those who are newly exposed to intelligence. What are they going to get from intelligence? What do policymakers understand about what they can and cannot expect from intelligence? What do state and local organizations understand about expectations that they should have?

The second issue is security. Security is a key determinant, obviously, in what is shared and how. Historically, we have had a principle known as the "need to know" principle, by which we shared sensitive information with the fewest possible number of people required to make a decision, to take an action, etc. Today, terrorism turns the "need to know" principle on its head because we may not know who needs to know a particular piece of information. There is an imperative to share—a need to share. However, we also have to be careful about specific problems in a "need to share" regime, such as the damage that insiders can do if improperly exposed to information that cannot be shared.

We have a conservative security culture in this country. New initiatives such as those recommended by the Markle Foundation suggest that rather than writing documents in a highly classified fashion, we start to write documents at the lowest possible classification level and add the sensitive data on top of that so that the broadest possible exposure can be given to the bulk of the information.

One of the issues that has not been focused on in the intelligence sharing domain is that if we have a need to share information, it is going to place an extraordinary premium on the development of new sources and methods and on the front end of the intelligence business. If you give a piece of information—or you create a piece of information and you are going to definitely share it—you are going to have to figure out a way to develop new sources of special kinds of information.

In the area of analysis, there are some particular issues with regard to intelligence sharing that we have to think about. Most of the focus on intelligence sharing has been about what I call the "pipes" issue: getting data from point A to point B. What we have little understanding of today, three years after 9/11, are the analytic issues associated with intelligence sharing. How do I, for example, overlay the buzz from the copy on the beat with a traditional piece of signals intelligence data or imagery intelligence data? How do you address data quality issues? How do you express confidence in a single piece of data? And then, lastly, how do you provide effective warning publicly?

The problem of providing warning is not a purely academic exercise. It involves tremendous cost, especially at the state and local level. We have to do a better job at doing the warning function. This is an area where there is very much room for a lot of theoretical work to be done, drawing from other examples for warnings such as earthquake warnings.

Let me conclude that a great number of efforts are under way. Many of them are focused on organization. Let me focus on two points in this regard. One, if we divorce the operational issues associated with counterterrorism from the broader themes that we have to understand—politics, economics, and culture—we will be in trouble. We are quickly moving into a world where there are a large number of people moving data around, but there are very few people who understand either the content or the context of that data, which is very important. We need to return our intelligence capability to a world of longer-term thinking, especially against an adversary who uses deception and noise against us very effectively.

A tremendous amount of work is going on in the intelligence community, not simply at the organization level but within organizations proper and even at what I might call the "seams" of organizations—things that are not as dramatic as organizational change but that are taking place between the agencies. Especially in the war on terror, we have to return to a basic concept of intelligence, which is that rather than moving data around about our adversary or reading a thousand messages a day about our adversary, we really have to return to an understanding of our adversary.

Lynn Davis

Thank you, Kevin. We've been mentioning the need to do analysis of terrorism, and perhaps that is the most difficult task that we face as we confront the issues ahead. Greg Treverton will give us his insights on this, having addressed intelligence issues on the Hill for the first Senate Select Committee on Intelligence.

Gregory Treverton

When I was at the National Intelligence Council (NIC), I used to take comfort in the fact that a prediction of continuity beats the best weather forecasters. So if it is raining, you say it is going to rain until the sun comes out; if it is sunny, you say it is going to be sunny until it starts raining. If weather forecasters with some theory and lots of data can't do any better than that, who could expect us to forecast the fall of the Soviet Union? It is precisely that analytic task to which I want to turn—connecting the dots and doing better in the analytic process against terrorism, both to understand the threat and to take advantage of opportunities.

The first thing that strikes you about the terrorist target is how different it is from the Cold War focus on the Soviet Union. Obviously there is some overlap between it and crises or military engagements, but it is a very different target.

Three points strike me about that difference. One is that we carry in our heads, policymakers or intelligence analysts, some story about what a state is. We have some idea about how states behave, even very different states. This is not true for nonstates—we have no story or models for how they behave. Second, nonstates may move faster—at least faster than the Soviet Union. Surely the terrorists are patient; we have seen that. But still we will see discontinuities in tactics and targets, even within groups. By contrast, we got used to a Soviet Union that was ponderous. As one Secretary of Defense said famously about Soviet responses to our nuclear weapons programs, "When we build, they build; when we stop, they build. So predictable." And given that terrorism is the ultimate tactic of the weak, the ultimate asymmetric threat, our actions matter more to determining that threat than was the case with the Soviet Union.

This means that analysis has to be done very differently. It is not a case of discrete products thrown over the transom, as was often the case during the Cold War. What is needed is a process of continuous updating, maybe somewhat more like military intelligence, where we are constantly updating the threat and opportunity against lots of uncertainty, with new information but still lots of uncertainty, in the knowledge that we could succeed or fail at any moment.

It is a process that University of Michigan psychologist Karl Weick calls "sense making"—not analysis but sense making.

The second change is, while terrorists do not exactly advertise their plans on the Internet, so secrets are still important, there is also lots of nonsecret information—DMV [Department of Motor Vehicles] records, for instance—lots and lots of it not very reliable, or, at least, information of very uneven quality.

In the process, the distinction between analysts and collectors that existed during the Cold War also begins to break down. The best person to be sifting through that stuff on the Net to sort out nuggets from all the chaff is an expert, somebody who knows the field—an analyst.

During the Cold War, intelligence analysts worked alone or in small groups, sometimes on very small accounts. That, too, has to change. The kinds of teams one needs to put together to understand the terrorist threat would range across theology, religious studies, and business—they would be very different kinds of teams. By the same token, the Intelligence Community has not traditionally made much use of either computers as assistance or of formal methods of analysis; that also has to change.

Our work on analysis developed a number of specific ideas. Let me just mention four to you.

(1) Greater use of formal methods and machines to extract hypotheses, to see patterns, and to sort through massive amounts of data. As an example, when I was at the National Intelligence Council in 1994, the CIA used a technique called factions analysis, which they still use. It is a method of putting together essentially subjective judgments. They did the factions analysis on the question of what it would take by way of U.S. action to make Milsosevic change his objectives, in this case in Bosnia. The median point of this analysis said that it would take military strikes on industrial targets in Serbia proper. This was 1994, when we at most were talking about thin peacekeeping in Bosnia. I sent it to my colleagues at the NSC saying, "Be careful; if you are going to get involved in military measures, it is going to be a serious fight."

(2) "Multi-int," these days one of the buzzwords in the community. It is a process of rapidly relaying information from various sources to try and see, in particular, tactical pictures. Imagine if the FBI office in Phoenix had been able to put what it knew two years before with what it knew in the summer of 2001. Again, there should be much more use of some formal methods and machines as an aid to analysis.

(3) Weblogs as a way to produce intelligence, duplicating the informality of conversation. Also, looking at the experience of the best Wall Street firms in analysis, they do what they call "barbelling," mixing fearless young people with good gray heads to organize analytic teams.

(4) After-action reports. It is striking that while the military does after-action reports almost all of the time, intelligence seldom does them and usually then as kind of a finger-pointing "whose-fault-was-it?" exercise. After-action reports ought to be done all the time with an interest in doing better and creating higher-performance organizations, rather than to determine who was to blame.

All of these ideas run into three enormous challenges for the community: consumers, organization, and secrecy.

Consumers. If the process is really "sense making" and not analysis, then consumers need to be much more involved. Intelligence cannot be developed apart and then passed to them. They need to be involved in the process. But consumers are too busy—busy all the time. So that is a real puzzle. We looked at a variety of ways of engaging policymakers—for instance, "RapiSims," table simulations they can do on their computers, and other ways to engage policymakers that aren't big drains on their time.

Organizations. The interesting innovations are going on around the edges of organizations, often called "edge organizations." Changing the organizational cultures of the big agencies will be an enormous task. To give you one particular, all the research says that creativity happens when people are slightly down, reflecting not running. But this is a community that all the time is running after the latest new factoid, the latest new tidbit, so creating the kind of space for reflection is no easy task. But it will be all the more necessary because if the community goes in the direction the 9/11 panel suggests—toward national intelligence centers, of which the National Counterterrorism Center is the prototype—it is almost inevitable that, like the military unified commands which is their model, they will be very dominated by the immediate. They can hardly be otherwise. It will take real leadership to build those centers but also then create counterweights like the NIC or other places around town that are not dominated by the urgency of the immediate.

Secrecy. The 900-pound gorilla. Interestingly, intelligence analysts are so used to it they hardly see that gorilla. But doing analysis of terrorism means precisely getting access to information for those who do not have a "need to know." They may see new patterns or new hypotheses that other people will not. One example of the security obstacles I have come to call "wheeled fusion." An analyst sitting inside the security fence at an installation literally wheels his or her chair between different screens with different information sources on them. It is, in the circumstances, an impressive innovation and adaptation, but it also demonstrates just how far we have to go in sharing information, even with ourselves.

Lynn Davis *is a senior political scientist at the RAND Corporation. Her current research focuses on terrorism, citizen preparedness, and Army strategic and force structure issues. From 1993 to 1997, Dr. Davis served as Under Secretary of State for Arms Control and International Security Affairs. She was the Senior Study Group Advisor for the recent Commission on National Security/ 21st Century.*

Prior to joining the State Department, Dr. Davis was vice president and director of the Arroyo Center at RAND. She has also served on the staffs of the Secretary of Defense, the National Security Council, and the first Senate Select Committee on Intelligence. She has taught at George-town University in the Security Studies Program, the National War College, and Columbia University. Her recent publications include a RAND occasional paper entitled Coordinating the War on Terrorism, *with Gregory Treverton et al.;* Individual Preparedness and Response to Chemical, Radiological, Nuclear, and Biological Terrorist Attacks *with Tom LaTourrette et al.; and* The U.S. Army and the New National Security Strategy, *edited with Jeremy Shapiro.*

Dr. Davis has a Ph.D. in political science from Columbia University.

Michael Wermuth *is a senior policy analyst at the RAND Corporation and Manager of Domestic Counterterrorism Programs in the RAND National Security Research Division. He has directed numerous projects dealing with homeland security, including the congressionally mandated Advisory Panel to Assess Domestic Response Capabilities for Terrorism Involving Weapons of Mass Destruction (the "Gilmore Commission"); a study for using military medical resources to assist civil authorities; a terrorism incident database and related analyses; a project to catalogue and analyze the authorities, roles, and missions of federal agencies for response to terrorist attacks; and the National Response Plan and National Incident Management System for the Department of Homeland Security.*

Mr. Wermuth has an extensive background in government, including service as Deputy Assistant Secretary of Defense for Drug Enforcement Policy, as Principal Deputy Assistant Attor-

ney General for Legislative Affairs, and as Chief Counsel and Legislative Director for Senator Jeremiah Denton.

His military experience, including both active and reserve duty with the U.S. Army, spanned more than 30 years before his retirement as a reserve colonel. He commanded at the company, battalion, and group level, and is a graduate of the U.S. Army Command and General Staff College and the U.S. Army War College. He is a recipient of the Secretary of Defense Award for Outstanding Public Service from then-Secretary Dick Cheney. He is listed in Who's Who in America *and* Who's Who in American Politics *and serves on the American Bar Association Standing Committee on Law and National Security.*

Mr. Wermuth received his B.S. in commerce and business administration from the University of Alabama and his J.D. from the University of Alabama School of Law. He is admitted to the practice of law in Alabama and the District of Columbia, and before several U.S. Courts of Appeal and the Supreme Court of the United States.

Kevin O'Connell *is Vice President for Intelligence Community Programs at the Defense Group Inc. He is the former director of the Intelligence Policy Center at the RAND Corporation, where he oversaw research efforts on behalf of the U.S. Intelligence Community. His professional interests include national security decisionmaking; strategic intelligence and intelligence-sharing issues; and the policy, security, and market issues related to commercial remote sensing. Mr. O'Connell serves on a number of senior government panels, including one related to the National Geospatial Intelligence Agency (NGA) and DARPA, and the Information Sharing and Collaboration Advisory Panel for the Department of Homeland Security (DHS). He also served as the executive secretary and staff director of the Independent Commission on the National Imagery and Mapping Agency (NIMA) (1999–2000).*

Mr. O'Connell joined the Department of Defense in November 1982 and served in various positions as a senior staff officer and intelligence analyst. In 1986, he joined the State Department's Bureau of Intelligence and Research as a research analyst. In 1990, he was assigned as the senior analyst in the White House Situation Room, National Security Council, and later served as a Special Assistant to the Vice President for National Security Affairs. From 1993 to 1995, Mr. O'Connell served on the Community Management Staff of the Director of Central Intelligence (DCI), where he was responsible for assessing nontraditional intelligence activities, including the DCI's Openness initiative.

Mr. O'Connell's recent research activities include various assessments of the state of U.S. intelligence, including collection, analysis, and intelligence-sharing issues, and has led a number of assessments on the market and security issues associated with remote sensing commercialization.

RAND and the American Society for Photogrammetry and Remote Sensing (ASPRS) published his edited volume, entitled Commercial Observation Satellites: At the Leading Edge of Global Transparency, *in 2000.*

Mr. O'Connell received a Sustained Superior Performance Award from the U.S. National Security Advisor for his work in the White House Situation Room. He received a Distinguished Speaker Award from the Department of Defense. He also received the Outstanding Service Award from the ASPRS in 2002.

Mr. O'Connell earned his B.A. in international studies from The Ohio State University and his M.P.P. from the University of Maryland.

Gregory Treverton *is acting director of the Intelligence Policy Center at the RAND Corporation, where he formerly directed the International Security and Defense Policy Center. He is also associate dean of the Pardee RAND Graduate School. Dr. Treverton's recent work has examined terrorism, intelligence, and law enforcement, with a special interest in new forms of public–private partnership. He has served in government for the first Senate Select Committee on Intelligence, handling Europe for the National Security Council, and, most recently, as vice chair of the National Intelligence Council, overseeing the writing of America's National Intelligence Estimates (NIEs).*

He holds an A.B. summa cum laude from Princeton University and an M.P.P. and Ph.D. in economics and politics from Harvard University. His most recent book is Reshaping National Intelligence for an Age of Information *(Cambridge University Press, 2001).*

CHAPTER SEVEN

Terrorism in Russia:
Preliminary Thoughts on the Beslan Attack

Olga Oliker

The Attack in Beslan

Several commentators, particularly Russian commentators, have characterized the early September 2004 hostage crisis in Beslan, Russia, when a group of armed terrorists took control of a school on the first day of classes, as Russia's "September 11": a "wake-up call." But if 9/11 was a wake-up call for the United States, Beslan might be better described as merely the latest indicator that Russia has been hitting the snooze button on terror for a while. Not only was this far from the first major terror attack in Russia, it was merely the most recent of an escalating series of attacks, including in Moscow, Russia's capital. In addition to Beslan, the beginning of September 2004 alone witnessed two airplane bombings and a bombing just outside a busy Moscow metro station (the bomber was reportedly deterred from entering the metro by security personnel visible at its entrance). Russia has also seen grisly hostage situations before, most notably in a hospital in Budyonnovsk, in Southern Russia, in 1995, and in a theater in Moscow just two years ago. Beslan may be the grimmest of Russia's recent experiences with terror, but it is only the latest.

So what is notable about this attack aside from its gruesomeness? A few things stand out. One is that this attack could be characterized as terror in its purest form. Terror by its nature targets innocent civilians in an effort to influence policy. An attack on schoolchildren and their parents and grandparents is in some ways the quintessence of this. That said, it is not the first time something like this has happened. There was a hostage incident in a school in Israel in 1974, for example. It is also likely to happen again. In the modern environment, we have seen terrorist tactics emulated by other terrorists, the spread of suicide bombing being one predominant example. From a terrorist's perspective, this attack was successful. Thus, it too will be emulated.

Another notable thing about Beslan was the negotiation process. The public, in Russia and abroad, was told that the hostage-takers were demanding Russian withdrawal from Chechnya. This is not a new demand, but could the hostage-takers really have believed that they could achieve such an aim? One could argue that they could. This argument would be based on the success of the 1995 hostage-taking in Budyonnovsk, which some believe was what broke the back of the Russian government, eventually forcing it to the negotiating table with the Chechen leadership, and to withdrawal (albeit short-lived) from the breakaway republic in 1996. However, there are flaws in this argument. The Budyonnovsk hostage-takers' immediate gain was simply safe passage out of the hospital and the town. If Russian withdrawal from Chechnya was linked to this attack, the link was indirect.

In this case, as the haphazard and ill-organized negotiations went on, it seemed that the terrorists in Beslan were not willing to accept much in the way of a solution, a clear difference from Budyonnovsk. They were not willing to exchange the children for adults. They were not willing to accept offers of safe passage. In fact, it is very likely the terrorists got what they wanted in Beslan—that their best-case scenario was this worst-case scenario of chaos, of many people killed. This is because chaos and death on this order, of this sort, sends a signal to the population as a whole that they are not safe and that their government cannot protect them. That was the purpose of the attack, and in this it was successful.

Another thing that is notable about Beslan is what it tells us about the Russian government and its campaign on terror. The Russians have focused on subduing Chechnya, which they see as the source of their terror problem. They have not paid that much attention, except in the immediate aftermath of attacks like this, to protecting the population or to making the attacks more difficult. This means that the terrorists are right—Russia cannot protect its population from attacks like this. The borders are porous; the infrastructure is not safe; what security measures are taken are fairly easily evaded. Despite continuing and mounting attacks, Russia either is not willing to or is not able to take this problem sufficiently seriously.

One aspect of this is that Russian forces are not trained effectively and are not capable of responding to such extreme situations. The Budyonnovsk experience, almost ten years ago, showed striking similarities to both the theater incident and Beslan: Security forces attacked the building in which hostages were held, exhibiting poor planning and coordination, and numerous civilians were killed and injured. In the 2002 theater incident, limited information combined with the use of a dangerous gas may have even more directly contributed to casualties among the hostages.

Unfortunately, the lesson Russian security forces may have taken from the theater incident was that any plan of attack was a poor idea. Certainly they did not appear to have any particular response plan in Beslan. In fact, it is reported that efforts to develop an approach were just being devised several days into the crisis. But it was too late. A bomb went off, apparently accidentally; shots were fired; and security forces rushed into the school alongside civilians who had been gathered nearby. The anarchy and chaos were to some extent a result of a failure by security forces to cordon off the public, some of whom were armed, as well as a lack of contingency planning, which might not have anticipated the particular evolution of events but which might have rendered authorities more capable of responding to the unexpected. Other problems included inadequate communications and command and control, which could have rendered more effective the various disparate forces deployed to the school—police personnel, Special Forces personnel, and others. Forces did not seem trained or prepared for situations of this sort. In short, there was no structure to support a variety of disparate forces in a single crisis environment, and the personnel had limited means of communicating with each other and no clear sense of who was and was not in charge. All of these are issues that planning and preparation could have mitigated, if not prevented entirely.

Response and Follow-Up

The Putin government's response to Beslan in the early days of the crisis was subdued but became increasingly volatile in the days that followed the tragic climax. Aside from continued disinformation regarding both casualties among the hostages and the make-up and structure of the terrorists responsible, the Beslan crisis was the springboard for a number of striking policy statements and announcements, ones that could lead one to believe that Putin may have viewed Beslan as something of an opportunity to advance his policy goals. First, he publicly linked Aslan Maskhadov, the exiled former president of Chechnya (the last to be elected in any election that could conceivably have been called free and fair), to the hostage-takers, even though there is no evidence to suggest involvement by Maskhadov and his team, who have consistently denounced violence against civilians. He similarly denounced all those who argued for moderation in the Chechen conflict, suggesting that moderation was tantamount to negotiating with "child-killers." In sum, he sought to tar with the same terror brush all who disagree with his Chechnya policy. Moreover, some of his post-Beslan statements could be viewed as an implicit threat to his neighbors. In stating that the Russian government would pursue terrorists anywhere, it seems likely he was sending a message to countries such as Georgia. Russia has accused Georgia of failing to be sufficiently tough with Chechen terrorists ostensibly on its soil in the past and has used this as a pretext for military action on its neighbor's soil. The goals of such policies may have less to do with Chechnya and terror and more to do with ensuring that post-Soviet neighbors retain a healthy respect for and fear of Russian power. This feeds into a broader policy of seeking to expand Russia's influence over neighbors' foreign and domestic policies. Beslan may prove an excuse for more actions along these lines.

In the context of Russian politics today, it is highly unlikely that Putin will take any blame for what went wrong in Beslan. The Russian security forces may take some blame and may take some steps to reorganize, but they probably will not have the resources or the capabilities to do enough. This has been what has happened in past cases: Lip service is paid to the need to do more, to be more effective, to build capabilities, but little is done—in large part due to resource constraints. Moreover, the policy debate in Russia regarding Chechnya and terror pays little attention to what is needed to fight terror at the tactical level and how to respond to the threat. Rather, it focuses on broader issues: Russia's overall policy toward Chechnya, Putin's domestic policy more generally, and the suppression of free speech and dissent in the country as a whole. Like the government, the Russian public is not ready to accept that the terror threat is likely to outlast any given Chechnya policy.

Thus, Putin will continue to use Beslan as an excuse, as an explanation of why his Chechnya policy is the only option. Brutal military and police campaigns in the breakaway region will continue, as will the support of puppet governments there, which have little control or support. There will be no negotiations.

This will backfire, and will continue the cycle. But the choices facing Russia are not easy ones. Russian withdrawal from Chechnya would lead to the same problems that Russian withdrawal from Chechnya has led to before: anarchy and disorder within Chechnya, with repercussions for all of Russia and beyond. Various groups, violent and less so, will contest power in the republic, and once again, the region will be an exporter of crime, disorder, and drugs into Russia. It also has the potential to develop as a base for various criminal and terrorist groups within that region as it becomes more lawless, creating a threat beyond Russia's borders. So, a simple Russian withdrawal from Chechnya would not solve the problem.

Neither would negotiations end the terror attacks. First of all, even if Moscow was willing to negotiate with terrorists, there is nothing Moscow could rationally or credibly offer these most extreme of extremists that would end the attacks. Even if there was, it is unlikely that any one group could deliver a broader cease-fire. Although Shamil Basaev's name often surfaces as playing a leading role in authorizing such atrocities, it is likely that there are a number of groups linked to Basaev and unrelated to him involved in these attacks. Information is scanty, but it is unlikely that there is a clear line of command such that any one leader can effectively speak for other groups.

Because the terrorists have distanced themselves from Maskhadov and his exiled colleagues, and vice versa, neither would negotiations with these more moderate groups yield a speedy end to terror. But negotiations with moderates could have some positive effects for the long term. They could support better will among the Chechen public and less willingness among them to harbor terrorists, less acquiescence to their methods, less of a tendency to excuse them as motivated by hardship and by the actions of Russian troops. If there are negotiations, and some recognition that there might be a negotiated solution (perhaps even a multinational solution) to the problem, it might be possible to limit the amount of support that the terrorists receive from the public in Chechnya and elsewhere. In the meantime, while most separatist leaders want to distance themselves from these attacks, they also want to spread the concept that the attacks are a direct result of Russian government policy and, thus, Moscow's fault. How effective that will be is not clear, but it does contribute to the hardening of positions on all sides.

Regardless, negotiations are unlikely. And even if they were likely, there would still be more terror attacks, for the hardliners will oppose any negotiated solution and seek to derail it—most likely with terror attacks to demonstrate that negotiations cannot succeed. Thus, Russia will have to learn how to prepare for such attacks and recognize that one of the duties of the state is to provide security for its people—because Russia is not providing security for its people today.

What do these events mean for the rest of us? We must recognize that attacking terrorism by eliminating one group or another is not actually going to eliminate the tactic itself. It will be taken up by the next group that thinks it can be used effectively. That is something to remember as the Putin government pursues its policy in Chechnya and as all of us, in the United States and in other countries, consider what our policies should be toward various terrorist groups and toward terrorist tactics.

The other thing that we might all take from this is that protecting against terrorism is a question of actually "protecting": protecting infrastructure, protecting borders, protecting facilities, including schools. A lot of countries have experience with this. Israel foils far more attacks than it fails to prevent—schools there have armed guards. Russia has apparently expressed some interest in cooperating with Israel. Other countries have experiences that can be of value, including Russia and the United States. We can learn from failures as well as successes.

This sort of cooperation will not be easy. Collaboration between the United States and Russia on terror has been sporadic. Police cooperation tends to go well if the United States or Russia can identify a suspect or a potential suspect. Then authorities in the other country will look into the specific case if requested. This is also how the cooperation on terrorism has developed. Authorities in one of the two countries discover information of some sort, which requires help from the other nation; they request that help; and the other country is generally cooperative. But the sort of day-to-day intelligence sharing and preventive long-term cooperation that is crucial to move beyond this has gone less well. There are a number of reasons for this, including the organizational secrecy of the agencies in question in both countries, as well as lingering distrust between the two states in a broader sense. The unwillingness of Russia to overtly request the assistance of the United States is another factor.

But the fact is that both the United States and Russia are facing a threat that is networked, that communicates, and that learns from the mistakes of others of its ilk. Therefore, we can and must learn from other nations' successes and failures as well, and we must learn to coordinate and cooperate. We have to learn how to protect people, and this is not just about surveillance and intelligence—it is also about protecting the facilities that are likely to be targeted. Red Team exercises can help understanding of what the likely targets will be, and how they might be attacked.

The other thing we need to think about is how to respond to situations like this one. How do you negotiate with people whose best-case outcome includes their own deaths? In the traditional hostage situation, there is a demand that is made, and the hostage-takers have an interest in keeping themselves and probably also the hostages alive and then getting what it is they want. In this case, what they are trying to do is demonstrate to the public at large that they are willing to stop at nothing, that they are willing to die themselves. The traditional mechanisms of negotiation, of offering money or safe passage, may well not be effective in this context.

What might be effective? Should those who seek to fight terror try convincing some of these people, who are the foot soldiers of the terrorist groups, that perhaps they do not want to die? Should they develop plans of attack for a variety of scenarios?

I would close by stressing the point that this is something we are likely to see again, both the attack on children and the willingness of the hostage-takers to die. So understanding how to protect against it is going to be crucial to fighting it.

Olga Oliker *is an international policy analyst at the RAND Corporation. Her research focuses primarily on U.S. foreign and defense policy; defense and security issues relating to Russia, Central Asia, and the Caucasus; and transnational security. Before coming to RAND, Ms. Oliker worked as an independent consultant and held positions in the U.S. Departments of Defense and Energy. In early 2004, she took some time away from her RAND research to serve as a special advisor for national security affairs to the Coalition Provisional Authority in Baghdad. Recent RAND publications include* Aid During Conflict: Interaction Between Military and Civilian Assistance Providers in Afghanistan, September 2001–June 2002 *(Olga Oliker et al., 2004),* Clean, Lean, and Able: A Strategy for Defense Development *(David C. Gompert, Olga Oliker, and*

Anga Timilsina, 2004), and Faultlines of Conflict in Central Asia and South Caucasus: Implications for the U.S. Army *(Olga Oliker and Thomas S. Szayna, eds., 2003).*

Ms. Oliker holds a B.A. from Emory University and an M.P.P. from the Kennedy School of Government at Harvard University.

CHAPTER EIGHT

Preventing Terrorist Use of Nuclear Weapons

Michael Hynes

It must be an overriding goal to prevent a nuclear detonation in the United States or in allied countries. Such a detonation would have profound effects: the human toll, economic dislocation, and societal-cultural consequences that could be hard to predict. The consequences of a biological or chemical attack pale by comparison.

Terrorist groups are seeking nuclear weapons, and there is increasing concern that these subnational groups may succeed. The availability of nuclear technologies, materials, and skilled personnel is widespread. Unconventional designs make nuclear weapons easier to build than many appreciate. Recent revelations about nuclear trafficking raise concerns about someone being able to buy a weapon or weapon materials.

To prevent the acquisition of nuclear capabilities by terrorists, four areas related to the development of nuclear weapons or their modification need to be monitored or controlled:

(1) Property, plant, and equipment (e.g., specialized machine tools, foundries and machine shops for nuclear materials and explosives, and specialized software design tools)
(2) Personnel with expertise in nuclear technologies and explosive technologies
(3) Special materials (e.g., weaponizable material and nuclear and nonnuclear components)
(4) Foreign arsenals of nuclear weapons (i.e., these must be made safe and secure).

The pathways for acquiring nuclear weapons are complex, as indicated on the chart on the following page.

Nuclear technologies, material, and personnel are internationally available. Nuclear reactors exist all over the world. Power and research reactors are widespread. While U.S., Russian, and Chinese designs tie the host country to the design country, some reactors are

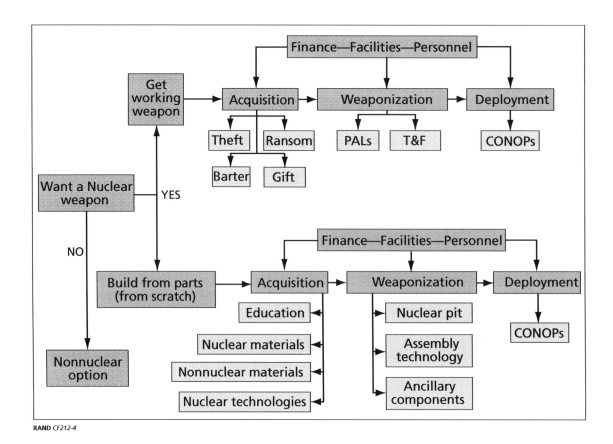

RAND *CF212-4*

Pathways for Acquiring Nuclear Weapons

local designs (e.g., DPRK). Moreover, many research reactors are in global trouble spots. Reactors and associated technologies also create a cadre of individuals skilled in the nuclear area. Fortunately, additional skill sets are needed to build a nuclear device. Unfortunately, control regimes such as the nuclear suppliers group are largely ineffective. International Atomic Energy Agency (IAEA) safeguard inspections have significant limitations, and alternative nuclear materials can be weaponized. Lastly, the security of Russian nuclear materials varies widely.

The illegitimate nuclear market is segmented into two elements: the visible market and the hidden. The participants in the visible market are typically low-ranking employees or amateurs. However, in the hidden market they are mid-level and senior government officials. When it comes to materials, the visible market deals mostly with radioactive "junk" unsuitable for making nuclear explosive devices. But in the hidden market, some weapon-grade and weapon know-how is available.

The nuclear market usually requires "brokering" mechanisms or middlemen. In the visible market, these often consist of spontaneous, unstable networks. The hidden market is the domain of criminal syndicates, government officials, and visiting scientists. The customers in the visible market are subnational groups, middlemen, and criminal syndicates. In the hidden market, one finds the nuclear threshold states, undeclared nuclear states, and, again, subnational groups.

Looking at the impact on terrorism, it seems clear that the visible market offers a low to moderate risk, while the terrorist threat from the hidden market is moderate to high.

How can these threats be managed? Market forces can be used to advantage in both markets, but the hidden market also requires deterrence.

There are several market forces that we can manipulate in the hidden market segment. We must convince buyers and sellers that nuclear forensics can reveal the source of nuclear materials and that transferring nuclear weapons and components will have grave consequences for them. It must be made clear that transfers will not provide real advantage over adversaries nor improve their position in the international system. They will not take buyers or sellers closer to their ultimate policy objectives.

There are also market forces that we can manipulate in the visible market segment. Both supply and demand sides of nuclear transactions seek middlemen as a hedge against asymmetric information—that is, ignorance. The need for such middlemen creates opportunities to infiltrate or conduct stings, use bait and switch techniques, or carry out other scams.

Fortunately, nuclear myths abound in this marketplace. The perpetuation of these myths can structure the market in ways that we want. The strength of these myths can be manipulated to drive actors from the market or make bad technical choices.

Many physical aspects of a nuclear weapon development or acquisition program are detectable. There are low to moderate levels of radioactivity. Special scattering and absorption of subatomic particles is characteristic of nuclear materials. An ionized air cloud exists near radioactive materials as well as characteristic temperature and heat emission.

Electromagnetic interference is generated from tests, for example, of firing devices. Special chemicals are present in the effluent from isotope separation facilities, which also use large amounts of electrical power. Finally, nuclear devices produce unique spectral responses to pulsed neutron sources and moderate-energy x-ray sources.

Many of the process aspects of acquiring and developing nuclear weapons are also detectable. This includes the recruitment and movement of personnel; the acquisition of knowledge and expertise as well as specialized equipment; and the acquisition and use of suitable facilities. All of this requires the creation and movement of financial resources that can be tracked.

How can the necessary detection and monitoring be done? Fortunately, there are many current and future sensors and sources of intelligence on nuclear programs. In addition to human intelligence, there are techniques to extract intelligence from the World Wide Web. Electro-optical, infrared, multispectral imaging sensors can be ground-based, spaceborne, or airborne, including micro-air vehicles and microbots. Radar (spaceborne, airborne) sensors are valuable for this mission, especially radar capable of penetrating foliage and the ground. Other means of intelligence collection are signal interception (spaceborne, airborne), chemical sensors (airborne, ground-based, microbots), acoustic seismic sensors (ground-based, microbots), and radiation detectors on conveyances, containers, portals, and microbots.

There are more opportunities to detect a nuclear weapon program in the early phases. This is illustrated in the graph on the following page.

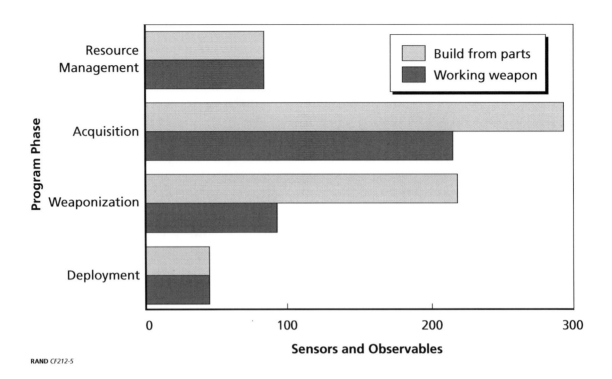

RAND *CF212-5*

There Are More Opportunities to Detect in the Early Phases of a Program

In sum, there are many ways of preventing terrorists' use of nuclear weapons:

(1) Convince them that nuclear weapons are too difficult or costly to acquire and use. Poison the market with disinformation. Use stings, bait and switch, and scams to disrupt the market.

(2) Strengthen international control regimes on transfers of specialized materials, equipment, and personnel to prevent leakage from legitimate to illegitimate markets. New control regimes must be developed for alternative material and technologies.

(3) Strengthen U.S. negative security assurances and incentives.

(4) Assure foreign stockpiles are safe and secure. Be willing to export U.S. security systems and expertise.

(5) Constantly scan existing sensor outputs and other intelligence sources for observables associated with nuclear weapon development programs. Develop and use data mining and inference systems for this task.

(6) Develop sensors specifically intended to search for nuclear weapon program observables.

Michael Hynes *is a senior physical scientist at the RAND Corporation, where he works on analyses associated with terrorism and homeland security. His work has examined how well prepared the Air Force is for its responsibilities in homeland security; has analyzed the legal basis for* *the domestic use of deadly force; and has continued to focus on nuclear terrorism. He has also worked on applying management practices from the private sector to organizational issues in the government sector.*

Dr. Hynes came to RAND in 1998 after 15 years at Los Alamos National Laboratory, where he conducted a wide variety of basic and applied research projects in the Nuclear Weapons Testing Program, and at nuclear and particle physics facilities around the world. He has served as a technical consultant to the Strategic Arms Reduction Talks and as the executive organizer of the Los Alamos Nonproliferation Task Force.

Dr. Hynes is the author of more than 50 publications in the refereed technical literature and has delivered 20 invited presentations at professional technical meetings. He is the author of several books and has written 15 classified articles and reports. Dr. Hynes has one patent and one patent pending.

Dr. Hynes received both his Sc.B. and Ph.D. in physics from the Massachusetts Institute of Technology (MIT) and his Sc.M. in management in 1991 from the Sloan School at MIT. In 1978, he was awarded the Weizmann Fellowship by MIT; in 1980, he received the Oppenheimer Fellowship from Los Alamos Scientific Laboratory; and in 1990, he received the Sloan Fellowship from MIT. He was the recipient of the Distinguished Performance Award from Los Alamos National Laboratory in 1993 and the Los Alamos Industrial Fellowship in 1994.

CHAPTER NINE
Building Counterterrorism Strategies and Institutions: The Iraqi Experience

Andrew Rathmell

The development of counterterrorism (CT) strategies and institutions by U.S. allies is a vital tool against terrorism. After Saddam's fall, Iraq had to start largely from scratch in developing CT strategies and institutions. At the same time, it faced a determined onslaught from terrorist and insurgent groups. In fact, Iraq has become perhaps the central front today in the campaign by al Qaeda terrorists against the United States.

How did the coalition and its Iraqi counterparts build strategies and institutions to counter terrorism? The answer to that question will help in understanding the achievements of coalition and Iraqi officials. It will illustrate the need for coordinated and multifaceted counterterrorism strategies. It will underscore the requirement for the United States and its allies to enhance their support of Iraq's counterterrorism effort.

It is crucial to recognize that success in the war on terrorism largely depends on our allies' own efforts. Therefore, it is important to optimize support for those efforts. Such assistance is not new. Foreign internal security assistance was a staple in the Cold War. The United States has been engaged in nation-building since the 1990s. Security and intelligence assistance has been stepped up since 9/11.

But successful counterterrorism involves more than the security forces. It requires an integrated, whole-of-government approach. It requires public support and engagement.

The Coalition Provisional Authority (CPA) developed a counterterrorism strategy and institutions as part of its preparation for the transfer of power to the Iraqi. This transition was taking place within a climate of violence by insurgents, organized criminals, and terrorists. The counterterrorism focus was on Sunni Islamist extremists that were a threat to the nation's stability and the security of the populace. All Iraqi factions agreed that they had to be neutralized.

Iraqi capabilities, however, were minimal. The security agencies had been removed from power. The police, armed forces, and intelligence services were still nascent.

47

A twin-track strategy was adopted. On the strategic level, a Ministerial Committee on National Security was used to formulate long-term strategy. On the operational level, preparations for the Shiite religious festival of Arbaeen in April, which was expected to involve up to a million people, were used to exercise the Iraqi government's CT machinery. Overall, we sought to coordinate existing programs as much as to spark initiatives. For instance, we sought to establish the legal basis for internal use of Iraq's armed forces and to develop a national command and control center.

The CT strategy had four key elements. The first priority was coordination and control. This involved creating a national focal point for policy development and coordination. The second was to build centralized analysis and coordination of the intelligence services. The third was to work toward international cooperation and to use diplomacy and liaison to reduce outside support for terrorists. The fourth element was public support. We wanted to assure Iraqi ownership of the strategy. These four elements were predicated on the assumption that strengthening the legitimacy of the government was as important as the attrition of terrorists.

The impact of the strategy was mixed. Implementation of the strategy was hampered by the need to meet immediate security demands and by the lack of Iraqi government capacity.

But there were major achievements. The security policymakers learned to work together in a structured way. Operational-level coordination was exercised and improved. Substantive progress was made in engaging the religious and educational establishments in the CT effort.

What can be learned from this experience? First, it is essential to ensure that counterterrorism strategies are comprehensive and proactive. The counteroffensive against the terrorists must be taken on the political, religious, and economic fronts, with security operations in support. Second, the focus must be on public support. It is essential to counter terrorist intimidation of the populace and concentrate on ameliorating the political, social, and religious roots of terrorism.

More specifically, it is important to prioritize domestic intelligence and investigation capabilities. There was too much focus on direct action and the use of military forces. We need to do better at helping to build effective, police-led domestic intelligence and investigative capabilities.

Much can be done to improve the ability of the United States and the United Kingdom to support our allies. Agencies in the coalition governments did not provide enough of the right people to staff their programs. Moreover, individual agencies did not link their programs to the broader strategy.

The following conclusions can be drawn from the Iraq experience. Iraq and its coalition partners developed a strategy, built policymaking and operational management mechanisms, and implemented elements of this strategy.

But the capacity of the Iraqi state to implement the CT strategy remains very limited. To help them overcome their deficiencies, we need a more determined commitment and to deploy enough experienced people from our governments to get this right in Iraq.

Andrew Rathmell *is director of RAND Europe's Defence and Security Programme. He has published many books, articles, and reports on Middle Eastern politics, intelligence, cyber-security,* *and risk management, including* Secret War in the Middle East *(I.B. Tauris, 1995),* The Changing Military Balance in the Gulf *(RUSI, 1996),* Protecting the Digital Society: A Manifesto for the UK *(IAAC, 2002), and* Engaging the Board: Corporate Governance and Information Assurance *(RAND, 2003).*

Prior to joining RAND, Dr. Rathmell was a Senior Lecturer in War Studies and director of a research center at London University; before that he held a research fellowship at Exeter University.

Major research projects that he has managed since coming to RAND in 2001 include the European Commission's Dependability Development Support Initiative (DDSI), which assisted the Commission in developing a comprehensive policy and research program on information infrastructure dependability; the European Commission's Handbook on Computer Misuse; and the Information Assurance Advisory Council, a UK public–private partnership for the development of information assurance policy and practices.

For six of the ten months that he served with the Coalition Provisional Authority (CPA) in Baghdad, Dr. Rathmell was its Director of Policy Planning, responsible for the CPA's strategic plan for the security and development of Iraq. He developed and coordinated strategic policy within the CPA, with the Coalition Forces, with national capitals, and with Iraqi institutions. He was particularly involved in the development of the Iraqi security sector and development of counterterrorist policies. In January 2004, Dr. Rathmell risked his life to protect others during a mortar and rocket attack in Iraq. He became the first non-American to receive the Office of the U.S. Secretary of Defense Medal of Valor.

Dr. Rathmell holds a Ph.D. in Middle Eastern terrorism from King's College London and was educated at Balliol College Oxford and George Washington University.

A STRATEGIC APPROACH TO THE CHALLENGE OF TERRORISM

Paul Wolfowitz, Deputy Secretary of Defense

Remarks as prepared for delivery to the RAND Corporation
Grand Hyatt Washington, Washington, D.C.
Wednesday, September 8, 2004

SOURCE: *http://www.defenselink.mil/speeches/2004/sp20040908-depsecdef0721.html*

Thank you, Jim [Thomson]. Tommy Franks and I once attended a briefing together here in town, in January. And he said, with an impish grin, that he always looks forward to the opportunity to leave Florida to come to Washington. Of course, the truth, as you all know, is that most of us in Washington look for the opportunity to leave here to go almost anywhere. And you're probably asking yourselves why you chose to come here to Washington and in the middle of Hurricane Frances, of all things. It must mean that RAND isn't any better at predicting the weather than any of the rest of us are.

Half a century ago, when [U.S. Air Force] General [Hap] Arnold set up the RAND Corporation, or at least so the legend goes, he put it in California so that it could be free of the influences of Washington and engage in independent thinking. In fact, my understanding is he directed RAND not to even come back with any results for the first year or two. He probably didn't plan on your predecessors spending most of that time on the beaches, but my guess is that's what a lot of them did. On a day like today, you probably wonder why you didn't stay there yourselves.

When I worked on the East Asian policy in the Reagan administration, as George Shultz's Assistant Secretary of State for the region and then later as Ambassador to Indonesia, I was struck at how helpful it was for me in that job to be working for an administration of Californians. You didn't have to explain to them why Asia was important or, as sometimes happened, even just how big it was or where it was. Secretary Shultz loved to illustrate it with a joke about a proper Boston lady. She was from the old Boston, the one where the Cabots spoke only to Lodges and the Lodges spoke only to God. She paid her first visit to San Francisco and was asked how she liked the city, and she said, "Oh, it's quite beautiful. But it's so far from the ocean." Shultz used it to illustrate the fact that when you sit in California, you recognize that there's another ocean and another whole frontier and another whole way of looking at American foreign policy. I always took that a little personally, as a native New Yorker. But I certainly learned about the importance of the Asia-Pacific region.

Unfortunately, on a more serious note, the whole country came to have a different appreciation of New York three years ago when the city was subject to a brutal attack on September 11, and its firefighters and policemen and mayor and citizenry in general responded with the courage and dedication to duty that has earned the admiration of the entire country.

Twice in the last century, the United States went to war against a totalitarian evil, first in a bloody war against nazism and fascism, and then later in the "long twilight struggle" that was the confrontation with totalitarian communism. Each time, we achieved victories of truly historic proportions, united with allies dedicated to halting the spread of the totalitarian menace. Each time we thought, with the evil eliminated, we could enjoy a long period of unbroken peace. Each time, we suffered rude awakenings.

This time, September 11, 2001, was our wake-up call.

With the cold-blooded murder of 3,000 Americans and citizens of many other countries, we were once again in the middle of a war we didn't look for. It found us. We learned in one shattering and horrific attack that evil remains on the loose. Like each past confrontation, the target is freedom itself.

Three days after the Twin Towers crumbled into dust, the president stood among the smoking ruins, and assured rescue workers, and the rest of the nation, that "the people who knocked down these buildings will hear from all of us soon." And Americans did fight back—for the same reasons Americans went to war in the past. During one of my recent visits to Capitol Hill, Senator Joseph Lieberman described it well, reminding us that when America goes to war, "it's not for conquest, it's not for imperial colonial plunder. It's for security and a principle that has driven American history from the beginning, which is freedom and democracy."

To be successful once again in defending our security and our freedom, four basic principles need to guide our strategy in combating terrorist fanaticism:

- We must recognize that the struggle will be a long struggle, not something we will win in three years or eight years or perhaps even decades. But, we will win it, even though victory will probably not be marked by anything as dramatic as the signing ceremony on the USS *Missouri* or the collapse of the Berlin Wall.

- We must use all the instruments of national power, including military force, but not solely or even primarily military force. Indeed, the different instruments of national power, including the "softer" ones, reinforce one another.

- This is a struggle that will be waged in multiple "theaters," including our own country. We cannot ignore any of these theaters, but we need to sequence our efforts so that we focus our energies in the right places at the right times.

- Perhaps most important, this is an ideological as well as a physical struggle. We must do more than simply kill and capture terrorists. We must, as the president said in his first State of the Union message after September 11, work to build a "just and peaceful world beyond the war on terror," particularly in the Muslim world, so that we can offer a vision of life and hope and freedom to counter the terrorists' vision of tyranny, death, and despair.

From the beginning, President Bush recognized that this fight would be long and difficult. Just five days after the attacks on New York and the Pentagon, the President said:

> This is a new kind of evil.... This war on terrorism is going to take a while. And the American people must be patient. I'm going to be patient.... [T]his will be a long campaign, a determined campaign; a campaign that will use the resources of the United States to win. They have roused a mighty giant. And make no mistake about it, we're determined.

On October 8, 2001, the day after Operation Enduring Freedom began in Afghanistan, Secretary Rumsfeld told reporters:

> [T]hese strikes [in Afghanistan] are part of a much larger effort against worldwide terrorism, one that will be sustained and which is wide-ranging. It will likely be sustained for a period of years, not weeks or months. This campaign will be waged much like the Cold War.... We'll use ... every ... resource at our command. We will not stop until the terrorist networks are destroyed. Regimes that harbor terrorists and their training camps should know that they will suffer penalties. Our goal is not one individual; it is not one group.

I was struck by Secretary Rumsfeld's reference to the Cold War. It was a dramatic contrast to those who suggested that "all" we had to do was to eliminate al Qaeda in Afghanistan. As daunting as that task was—and it seemed even more formidable at the time Don Rumsfeld was speaking—it was nothing compared to the tasks that he laid out for us.

But indeed the problem does extend far beyond Afghanistan—to other states that harbor terrorists and use terrorism as an instrument of policy, to ungoverned areas where terrorists can find safe harbor and even to our own country and other free societies, where terrorists hide in plain sight.

And it extends far beyond al Qaeda, as dangerous as that organization is. In fact, one of the lessons of 9/11 is that terrorism is something we can no longer continue to live with as an evil but inescapable fact of international life, the way we did over the previous two or three decades. We can no longer tolerate a terrorist capacity to inflict thousands of casualties in a single conventional attack or hundreds of thousands of casualties if terrorists gain access to the most terrible weapons human beings have invented. We may not be able to eliminate every individual terrorist, but we can hope to eliminate global terrorist networks and end state sponsorship of terrorism. We can hope to see the ideologies that justify terrorism discredited as thoroughly and made as disreputable as ideologies as nazism is today. We can hope to see the bombing of churches denounced by Muslim leaders, as it was in Iraq last month, or the slaughter of schoolchildren universally condemned.

Americans have a reputation for impatience. That is a strength as well as a weakness. In this struggle, as in the Cold War, we may be impatient for results. But, looking at the stakes, we should recognize that we're in this fight for the long haul. It's striking in hindsight to look back at how quickly we became impatient with the situation in Europe just six months after the elation that greeted the end of the Second World War.

People were heard to say, "We've lost the peace." In his speech last week, the president mentioned a *New York Times* article that reported in 1946 that "in every military headquarters, one meets alarmed officials doing their utmost to deal with the consequences of the occupation policy that they admit has failed." Astonishingly, *Life* magazine was able to write, also in 1946: "We have swept away Hitlerism, but a great many Europeans feel that the cure has been worse than the disease."

Sometimes it's hard to remember how long it took to begin to turn around the situation in Europe. A full two years after the end of the war in Europe, President Harry Truman courageously proposed the Marshall Plan. Its purpose: to help the battered continent dig itself out of the economic catastrophe that was feeding the forces of communist totalitarianism. As late as the communist takeover of Czechoslovakia in 1948, people in the West were still debating whether there was even a threat that we needed to confront. And the idea that we would eventually win that struggle, after an effort that would extend over four decades, was something that few besides George Kennan dared to predict.

So too, today, a problem that grew up in 20 or 30 years is not going away in two or three. So, we must be resolved and patient. Our adversaries have demonstrated remarkable patience. They might be looking at Afghanistan, for example, and thinking: "It took us 10 years to drive the Soviets out; the Americans have been there less than 3."

But we know how Europe's story ends. We know it can be done—when leaders are determined to persevere ... when the American people and its allies are resolved to stand firm for freedom.

Freedom is the glue of the world's strongest alliances and the solvent that has dissolved tyrannical rule. The same values that held the Allies together over the course of four decades of often contentious debates are the values that have brought some 40 countries into the Coalition effort in Afghanistan, more than 30 countries with us into Iraq, and some 80 or 90 countries into the larger coalition against global terrorism. The longing for freedom that penetrated even the Iron Curtain was what brought about the peaceful end to the Cold War. That same universal desire for liberty—among Muslims as well as non-Muslims—will be our strongest weapon in fighting fanaticism today.

Our enemies know us by our love of liberty and democracy. We know them by their worship of death and their philosophy of despair. We were given a window into their dark and barren world when we intercepted a letter from an al Qaeda associate in Iraq to his colleagues in Afghanistan. Abu Musab al-Zarqawi, a major terrorist mastermind, gives us an idea of how they view the benefits of a free and open society emerging in the heart of the Middle East. "Democracy" in Iraq, Zarqawi writes, "is coming" and that will mean "suffocation" for the terrorists. He talks disparagingly about Iraqis who "look ahead to a sunny tomorrow, a prosperous future, a carefree life, comfort and favor." For Zarqawi, prosperity and happiness are inconsistent with the terrorists' mission. "We have told these people"—meaning Iraqi Muslims—Zarqawi writes, "that ... the nation cannot live without the ... perfume of fragrant blood spilled on behalf of God and that people cannot awaken from their stupor unless talk of martyrdom and martyrs fills their days and nights."

In the contempt he displays for whole groups of human beings, including Muslim Kurds and Muslim Shi'a, Zarqawi calls to mind the racism of the Nazis. And his glorification of death and violence also calls to mind the tyrannical movements of the last century. While he claims a mantle of religion, his rhetoric recalls the death's head that Hitler's SS proudly displayed on their uniforms.

But the great majority of human beings, Muslims along with everyone else, want to embrace life and freedom, if given the chance. Indeed, a few months back, Hamid Karzai said that if they registered 6 million to people to vote, he'd consider it a success. Currently, 10.5 million people are registered. In Iraq, the early caucuses for the Iraqi National Conference were met with an almost overwhelming number of Iraqis interested in serving Iraq. In Kut, more than 1,200 people competed for 22 seats; in Najaf, 920 candidates vied for 20. Thus, just like nazism and communism, this latter-day brand of totalitarianism contains the seeds of its own decay. But it will not collapse simply of its own weight. We must go on the offense.

Our offensive of necessity involves many and varied fronts. Not just different geographical theaters, though there are many of those. And not even primarily military fronts. This struggle is not just about killing and capturing terrorists, although that's critically important. More than three-quarters of al Qaeda's key leaders and facilitators have been killed. We will never know how many September 11th's have been prevented by intercepting the plotters and facilitators who have been killed or captured in the three years since.

The successes of the last three years have disrupted or prevented a large number of terrorist plans. But we can be virtually certain that there are still people out there plotting major attacks against us. Even capturing or killing bin Laden will not eliminate al Qaeda much less other terrorist groups.

While we cannot concentrate our efforts on only one front at a time, we also can't afford to put equal effort into each simultaneously. We need to sequence our efforts in a way that makes sense, recognizing also that what we do in one theater has impacts on others. We cannot have an al Qaeda strategy by cutting aid to, and thereby isolating, a country like Pakistan, for example, which is what happened in the 1990s. At the same time, success in one theater can provide a platform for success in others. Success in Afghanistan has not only deprived al Qaeda of a sanctuary there; it has also supported President Musharraf's bold position as a friend of the United States, and drove al Qaeda terrorists into Pakistan, where it has been possible to capture them. The capture of terrorist operatives in Pakistan has led to the arrests of key associates in places as distant as London and Chicago, and provided significant new information about terrorist plans.

Terrorists once found Saudi Arabia a friendly place to find money. But since the suicide bombings in Riyadh on May 12, 2003, it's been a far less hospitable place. The Saudis have been able to kill or capture more than 600 al Qaeda associates. And their counterterrorist efforts have benefited substantially from the ability of the United States to remove the threat of Saddam Hussein as well as the burden of supporting a large military presence on Saudi territory, which was made possible by the liberation of Iraq.

Morocco, Egypt, Algeria, the UAE [United Arab Emirates], Oman, Yemen, and other nations in the Arab world are giving us valuable cooperation. Uzbekistan, where we are encouraging internal political and economic reforms, is also a key state in the war on terror.

Indonesia, with the largest Muslim population of any country in the world, faces the challenge of terrorism at the same time that it is struggling to build new democratic institutions. For Indonesians, the attacks in Bali and Jakarta were their equivalent of September 11, and they have taken serious steps to deal with their own terrorist problem.

The Palestinian-Israeli problem is another theater in this struggle. President Bush has laid out the very clear solution to that problem, the establishment of two states, living side by side in peace. Getting to that solution is an enormous challenge. But getting there will be [sic] enormous benefits for our other efforts.

It's been said that diplomacy without military capability is nothing more than prayer. Brave American troops are performing their roles magnificently, giving our diplomacy enormous credibility. In other theaters, our diplomacy has been strengthened by military success. Not long ago, Libya saw what was happening in the region and agreed to peacefully dismantle its weapons programs.

For our military forces, the two central fronts are Afghanistan and Iraq. Today, in those two countries, 50 million people have been freed from brutal tyranny. Afghanistan and Iraq are on the way to becoming America's newest allies in the fight for freedom.

In Afghanistan, the Taliban has been overthrown and replaced by a new constitution and government, more representative of all the people than at any time in the country's history.

In Iraq, the government is under Iraqi control. Children no longer learn by textbooks that teach, "2 Saddams plus 2 Saddams equals 4 Saddams." And substantial progress is being made even in the face of an enemy who continued to fight long after the liberation of Baghdad, along with Zarqawi and its other terrorist allies, to prevent the emergence of a free Iraq. In Afghanistan, too, progress is being made despite the unwillingness of the Taliban to accept defeat.

Both Afghanistan and Iraq are moving with determination toward self-government. For terrorists, including associates of al Qaeda, the success of democracy in both countries will represent a major defeat.

There are those who debate whether Iraq was the right place to use military force. I agree with Senator John McCain who recently said, "Our choice wasn't between a benign status quo and the bloodshed of war. It was between war and a graver threat."

As the senator explained further, "There was no status quo to be left alone. The years of keeping Saddam in a box were coming to a close. The international consensus that he be kept isolated and unarmed had eroded to the point that many critics of military action had decided the time had come again to do business with Saddam, despite his near daily attacks on our pilots, and his refusal, until his last day in power, to allow the unrestricted inspection of his arsenal."

The success of democracy in Iraq is the terrorists' greatest fear—"suffocation," as I mentioned Zarqawi calls it. For success in Iraq will have effects far beyond its borders. As Senator McCain said, "Our efforts may encourage the people of a region that has never known peace or freedom or lasting stability that they may someday possess these rights."

When they possess those rights, it will be one more step in pushing the extremist ideology they espouse to the margins of civilized society. As the president said last week, "The terrorists know that a vibrant, successful democracy at the heart of the Middle East will discredit their radical ideology of hate. They know that men and women with hope and purpose and dignity do not strap bombs on their bodies and kill the innocent."

Winning in Iraq and Afghanistan is imperative, but it is only part of the larger war on terrorism. Winning in each of the geographical theaters I've mentioned is only part of the victory. Victory in the war on terror requires sowing the seeds of hope, expanding the appeal of freedom, particularly in the broader Middle East. That is why, in his speech marking the

20th anniversary of the National Endowment for Democracy last November, the president said that we must work with our partners in the Greater Middle East and around the world to promote tolerance, rule of law, political and economic openness, and the extension of greater opportunities so that all people—men and women alike, Muslim and non-Muslim—can realize their full potential.

As democracy grows in the Middle East, it becomes easier for peacemakers to succeed throughout the region. There are so many wonderful Muslims who are our best allies in fighting this ideological battle. They are not just Muslims, they are devout Muslims, and we need to use a terminology that doesn't put them on the other side—to our people or to theirs. Let me tell you briefly about three I know personally.

One of them is the new prime minister of Pakistan. Another one is the former president of Indonesia. The third is the former deputy prime minister of Malaysia, who was released last week, having served six years in jail as a political prisoner.

These are three of the most wonderful human beings in public life anywhere. It is men and women like them who will lead change throughout the Muslim world.

Of course, there will be skeptics, like those who reported from Europe in 1946. They will say, "It can't be done" and "Arabs don't do democracy." But I remember a time, some 20 years ago, when I worked for President Reagan on East Asian and Pacific matters, first as his Assistant Secretary of State for that region, and then as his ambassador to Indonesia, the country with the largest Muslim population in the world.

Back then, people said that the Philippines could do no better than the dictator they had, Ferdinand Marcos. People said that the Koreans and Chinese didn't care about freedom, or that their Confucian heritage predisposed them to tyranny, or that they were incapable of democracy because they had no historical experience with it. Those assertions ran counter to what President Reagan believed. As he put it in an historic address to the British Parliament in 1982, "It would be cultural condescension or even worse to say that any people prefer dictatorship to democracy."

In the Philippines, Ronald Reagan and Secretary of State George Shultz initiated a persistent effort to prod Marcos to embrace democratic change. Supported by America's firm insistence, the Philippine people finally forced Marcos to step down in 1986—helping turn that country from dictatorship to democracy. The following year, we saw a similar development in South Korea. Not long after that, Taiwan began to demonstrate that Chinese people, too, craved freedom and democratic self-government.

And we may well remember the democracies emerging from the shadow of communism in Central and Eastern Europe ... today moving forward to build free institutions and representative self-government. Like the recovering societies who stepped forward in 1949 to join NATO against Soviet expansion, countries like Poland, Hungary, the Czech Republic, along with seven other democracies of Central Europe, have also joined NATO. And they've become active contributors in the Balkans, in Afghanistan, in Iraq, and in the broader war against terrorism.

The president tells a story about the power of liberty ... about how President Truman and the American people believed after the Second World War that a free society could help turn Japan from an enemy in war to an ally in peace. And about how, today, he and Japan's Prime Minister Koizumi can sit down and talk about how to the keep the peace in the Korean peninsula, or in Iraq. "What's going to happen someday," said the president, "is that an American president is going to sit down with a duly elected leader of Iraq to talk about peace. And our children and grandchildren will be better off."

Just as in the years after World War II, victory will require great risk and sacrifice, and much hard work. The three Muslim leaders I mentioned earlier have risked their reputations, their freedom, and even their lives to stand up for freedom and democracy and religious tolerance. President Hamid Karzai in Afghanistan knows that his life is at risk every day for the cause that he believes in.

Thousands of Iraqis are signing up to join the new army and national guard and police force, knowing that they are risking their lives for the cause of a new Iraq. On my recent visit to Iraq, I met with a young Marine whose life had been saved by five members of the Iraqi National Guard, who risked their own lives to rescue him when he was wounded under fire. I met with the president of Iraq, whose predecessor on the Governing Council was assassinated by a suicide car bomb. I met with the deputy prime minister, who was the target of an assassination attempt by al Qaeda–associated terrorists two years ago in Northern Iraq. I met with Prime Minister Ayad Allawi, who was almost chopped in half by an ax wielded by one of Saddam's assassins in his apartment in London 25 years ago.

We met with the very impressive Sunni Arab governor of the province of Nineveh, Osama Kashmoula, who was tragically assassinated a month later. These Iraqis know what they are fighting for, and they understand the risks. Hundreds of Iraqi soldiers and police and national guardsmen have already given their lives in this cause. But as one young woman, whose sister had recently been murdered because she was working for a free Iraq said to us: "My father said, you must never back down in the face of evil."

These people are not retreating in the face of evil, and they have the support of extraordinarily brave young Americans who are risking their lives so that other people can enjoy freedom and so that our own people can live in greater security.

American servicemen and -women have fought bravely in battle to protect us, and in the process, they've liberated 50 million souls. They've labored with courage and decency and honor, helping Afghans and Iraqis heal the countries that were broken long before they arrived. We mourn each one of those Americans who have been lost for this cause. My friend Joe Lieberman put it eloquently when he said recently that "those who have given their lives have given them for a noble cause, a cause as critical to American security as most any I can think of that we fought over the centuries."

A couple of months ago, I was privileged to be present when a group of wounded heroes from Iraq, men and women, met President Bush at the White House. There was also a delegation of Iraqi women who are active leaders in helping Iraq build a new free society. They'd come to Washington to learn more about elections and government in a democratic society. When they met the Americans who'd been their liberators, they embraced them, and they thanked them over and over, through tears of joy. And one Iraqi woman summed up the feeling of the group this way: There would have been no opportunity, she said, for Iraqi women to learn about democracy were it not for the sacrifice of American servicemen and -women.

I recently got to know one American hero who helped give them that opportunity, an extraordinary young man, Army Sergeant Adam Replogle. He was fighting Sadr's army with his unit in May near Karbala. An RPG [rocket-propelled grenade] slammed into him, and he lost his left arm and the sight in his left eye. Adam put his enormous sacrifice into perspective this way. He said, "We're fighting for everything we believe in. We've freed Iraqis from a dictator who was killing Iraqis by the millions."

Sergeant Replogle described how he'd personally changed so many lives in Iraq, how he'd helped destroy terrorist cells and get people back into their houses, how he and his fellow soldiers helped multiply the numbers of schools in his sector from 2 to 40 in just a year. He'd even bought bikes for Iraqi girls and boys. "After all," he said, "they only cost five bucks, and these kids didn't have anything."

Sergeant Replogle summed up the situation like this: "Saddam affected everyone in that country." And he added, "Something had to be done."

Something had to be done, and Americans did it, just as Americans have always stood up to evil. There are others in the Muslim world who will one day join us as allies in this fight. That's because history has shown that, in their hearts, most people are steadfastly unreconciled to tyranny. So hope remains. As the president reminded us: "As freedom advances, heart by heart, and nation by nation, America will be more secure and the world more peaceful."